A Linguistics Workbook

A Linguistics Workbook

Ann K. Farmer
Richard A. Demers

Fourth Edition

The MIT Press
Cambridge, Massachusetts
London, England

This book was set in Univers and
Times New Roman by Asco
Typesetters, Hong Kong and was
printed and bound in the United
States of America.

Excerpt from *A Clockwork Orange* by
Anthony Burgess reprinted by
permission of W. W. Norton &
Company, Inc. and William Heinemann
Ltd. Copyright © 1963 by W. W.
Norton & Company, Inc. Copyright
© 1962 by Anthony Burgess.

Part II, Chamber Music, phonetically
transcribed, from *Collected Poems* by
James Joyce. Copyright 1918 by B.
S. Huebsch, Inc. Copyright 1927,
1936 by James Joyce. Copyright
1946 by James Joyce. Reprinted by
permission of Viking Penguin Inc.

ISBN 0-262-56143-3

10 9 8 7 6 5 4 3

Contents

4 Syntax

5 Semantics

6 Language Variation

7 Language Change

8 Pragmatics

9 Psychology of Language

Appendixes

Bibliography

Preface

Our goal in preparing the fourth edition of this workbook has remained essentially the same as in preparing the earlier editions: to offer students experience with a broader range of languages than is provided in *Linguistics: An Introduction to Language and Communication. Linguistics* focuses for the most part on the properties of English. As stated there, the main reason for this is that "it is essential that students be able to evaluate critically our factual claims at each step, for this encourages a healthy skepticism and an active approach toward the subject matter" (p. xii). Given that students have at least some command of English, we can assume that they are able to draw upon this knowledge to formulate, test, and revise linguistic hypotheses. Thus, they are introduced to the basic methodology of linguistics as a science.

Nevertheless, it is extremely important that students become familiar with the structural properties of languages other than English. In *A Linguistics Workbook*, therefore, we have provided exercises based on a wide variety of the world's languages. We have preserved most of the exercises from earlier editions, though we have dropped some and have added a few new ones. We have also revised several on the basis of our experience in using these exercises in the university classroom.

In general, we continue to work toward improving the clarity of the exercises and broadening the scope of the workbook in terms of languages covered. In several chapters we have selected material from particular languages because they illustrate a desired range of structural types. We invite students to look for similarities and common themes amid the structural diversity. In this way they begin to carry out one of the central goals of current linguistic theory: to discover the basic and shared organizing principles of human language.

As in the earlier editions, the chapters follow the order of presentation in *Linguistics*; thus, the chapter on morphology precedes the chapters on phonetics, phonology, and syntax. We prefer this order for two reasons. First, students have little difficulty relating to words, as opposed to perhaps less intuitively obvious units such as phonetic variants and distinctive features. Second, words encode not only morphological information but also phonological, syntactic, semantic, and pragmatic information; thus, the word can serve as an intelligible and unintimidating introduction to some of the basic concepts of linguistics.

This edition of the workbook also follows the earlier ones in that several of the exercises in the chapter on pragmatics would traditionally be placed in a syntax section. Even though these exercises require the student to recognize certain syntactic properties and regularities, we have placed them in the chapter on pragmatics in order to illustrate the numerous ways in which the major moods can be marked in the world's languages. In our exercises on moods we have also included examples of sentence negation, since negation frequently patterns with mood marking.

The exercises in this workbook vary in difficulty. This range makes the workbook appropriate for use in intermediate linguistics courses as well as introductory ones. The more difficult exercises also serve another purpose. There are frequently students who become extremely interested in linguistics and wish to do extra work. We have found that many of these exercises are both challenging and stimulating for such students.

We should also call attention to the following point. When one is dealing with a large number of languages, the problem of consistency across writing systems becomes very complex. For example, the symbol *a* (print-*a*) is typically used in texts to represent a lax low back vowel. In phonetic writing systems, however, the symbol for a lax low back vowel is *a* (script-*a*). We have nevertheless represented almost all of the low back vowels as *a*, in conformity with standard (not phonetic) convention. Unless otherwise noted, the user of this workbook should assume that the symbol *a* represents a lax low back vowel. Where appropriate, we have used International Phonetic Alphabet (IPA) symbols in place of the Smith-Trager transcription system used in the earlier editions. This change in transcription is consistent with the adoption of the IPA transcription system in *Linguistics*.

Finally, linguists are fond of saying that the best way to learn about linguistics is to *do* linguistics. This workbook is intended to make doing linguistics possible at an introductory level. We hope that students will find the exercises both interesting and instructive.

Acknowledgments

Many people have been involved in the preparation of this workbook. First, we would like to thank those who contributed the basic ideas for our preliminary versions of exercises: Jonathan Beck (French, 3.9, 3.10); Lee Bickmore (Korean, 3.2); Kathy Budway (Spanish, 2.3); Ken Hale, who helped us with the Dyirbal (4.13), Irish (4.16), and Navajo (8.12) exercises; Barbara Hollenbach (Copala Trique, 8.10); and Adrienne Lehrer, who suggested the idea behind the Indo-European exercises (7.1, 7.2).

We would also like to thank the following people who checked particular exercises and data for us: Julia Annas (British English, 6.2); Adele Barker (Russian, 1.8, 4.23); Jim Cathey (Finnish, 8.9); Christiane Dechert (German, 4.9); Hiroko Ikawa (Japanese, 4.24); Rich Janda (assisted by Sue Foster), who first used the original version of the British dialect story (6.2) as an exercise at the University of Arizona; Eloise Jelinek (Yaqui, 4.12); Margaret Jeun (Korean, 3.2); Soowon Kim (Korean, 3.2); the late Steve Lapointe and his students (Japanese, 4.24); Stan Lekach (Russian, 1.8, 4.23); Bruce Peng (Mandarin Chinese, 8.11); Sirpa Saletta (Finnish, 8.9); Kyung-Hee Seo (Korean, 3.2); Amy Sung (Korean, 3.2); Natsuko Tsujimura (all the Japanese exercises); Virginia Valian (1.5); Mary Willie (Navajo, 8.12); Moira Yip; and Ofelia Zepeda (Tohono O'odham, 1.6, 1.7, 3.3, 4.11).

Ken Hale and Donna Jo Napoli deserve special thanks for reading an earlier version of this workbook in its entirety and making valuable suggestions.

We would like to thank Mark Farmer for the drawings that appear throughout the workbook.

We are grateful, once again, to Anne Mark for her continued role as copy editor. We always rely on her skill and informed feedback to bring this project to successful completion.

Finally, we thank the many students who worked on various versions of these exercises. We have continued to improve the exercises, and to add new ones (and even delete some), based on our students' invaluable input. We would like to think that they learned positive things about linguistics in spite of the fact that the preliminary drafts of virtually all of the exercises needed subsequent refining.

1 Morphology

Name _____

Section _____

1.1 A Clockwork Orange: *Meaning and Form in Context*

The passage below is taken from Anthony Burgess's novel *A Clockwork Orange*. Many of the vocabulary items are borrowed (loosely) from Russian. First read the passage, trying to match the "new" words (underlined) with the definitions given in question A. Both structural (syntactic and morphological) clues and context will be helpful in figuring out what the words mean. Then answer questions A and B.

There was me, that is Alex, and my three <u>droogs</u>, that is Pete, Georgie, and Dim, Dim being really dim, and we sat in the Korova Milkbar making up our <u>rassoodocks</u> what to do with the evening, ... The Korova Milkbar was a milkplus <u>mesto</u>, and you may, O my brothers, have forgotten what these <u>mestos</u> were like, things changing so <u>skorry</u> these days and everybody very quick to forget, newspapers not being read much neither. Well, what they sold there was milk plus something else. They had no licence for selling liquor, but there was no law yet against <u>prodding</u> some of the new <u>veshches</u> which they used to put into the old <u>moloko</u>, so you could <u>peet</u> it with <u>vellocet</u> or <u>synthemesc</u> or <u>drencrom</u> or one or two other <u>veshches</u> which would give you a nice quiet horrorshow fifteen minutes admiring <u>Bog</u> And All His Holy Angels And Saints in your left shoe with lights bursting all over your <u>mozg</u>. Or you could <u>peet</u> milk with knives in it, as we used to say, and this would sharpen you up ... and that was what we were <u>peeting</u> this evening I'm starting off the story with.

Questions

A. Match each underlined word in the text with one of the definitions on the right, as shown in the first example. (Note: N = noun, V = verb, Adv = adverb)

Word

Definition

1. ___droog_____   friend (N)

2. _____   God (N)

3. _____   a drug* (N)

_____

_____

4. _____ thing (N)

5. _____ quickly (Adv)

6. _____ mind (N)

7. _____ place (N)

8. _____ milk (N)

9. _____ to produce (V)

10. _____ to drink (V)

11. _____ brain (N)

*These three words are probably *not* borrowed from Russian.

B. Provide morphological evidence (and syntactic evidence as well, if you can) to support your choices in question A. The first space is filled in as an example.

   1. *droog*. Evidence that *droog* is a noun: (Morphological) The plural *-s* is attached to *droog*. (Syntactic) *Droog* occurs in the phrase *my three droogs*. Nouns combine with possessive pronouns (*my, his*) and adjectives (*three, red, happy*) to form noun phrases.

   Context suggests that *droog* refers to Alex's companions. The definition most compatible with *droog*, then, is "friend."

   2.

   3.

4.

5.

6.

7.

8.

9.

10.

11.

1.2 Open- and Closed-Class Words

Read the following passage. For each underlined word, answer questions A–E. (A review of pages 19–23 and 42–46 of *Linguistics* will be helpful.) The answers to the questions for the word *meaning* are given as an example.

... almost <u>self-evidently</u>, a style is specific: its <u>meaning</u> is part and parcel of <u>its</u> period, and cannot be <u>transposed</u> innocently. To see other *periods* as mirrors <u>of</u> our own is to turn history <u>into</u> <u>narcissism</u>; to see other *styles* as open to our own style is to turn history <u>into</u> a dream. But such, really, is the dream of the pluralist: he seems to <u>sleepwalk</u> in <u>the</u> museum. (Foster 1982)

Questions

A. Is the word an *open-class* or *closed-class* word?

B. Is the word *simple* or *complex*?

C. For each complex word, identify its pieces. That is, does it have a prefix or a suffix? If it has a suffix, is the suffix inflectional or derivational?

D. What category (part of speech) does the word belong to?

E. What morphological evidence can you provide to support your answer to question D?

1. *meaning.* (A) open-class word; (B) complex; (C) *mean + ing* (stem + suffix), *-ing* is derivational; (D) *meaning* is a noun; (E) *-ing* attaches to verbs to create nouns. Note that an *-ing* morpheme does attach to verbs to create verbs (e.g., *walk + ing* as in *John was walking the dog*). We know, however, that the *-ing* in *meaning* is a noun-forming suffix rather than a verb-forming suffix because the plural morpheme *-s* can be attached to it: *its meanings are part and parcel of its period*. The plural morpheme cannot be attached to *walking*: **John was walkings the dog*.

2. self-evidently

3. its

4. transposed

5. narcissism

6. into

7. sleepwalk

8. the

Name _____

Section _____

1.3 Compound and Noun Phrase Ambiguities

English words can combine to form compound words, sometimes referred to simply as *compounds* (such as *car-phone*, *windmill*, *golf club*). (For discussion of compounds, see *Linguistics*, pp. 32–35 and 50–52.) A major indicator that a sequence of two words is a compound is that the relative prominence (emphasis, stress) occurs on the first word. Consider the words *green* and *house*. The sequence *green house* is a compound if *green* is emphasized (represented here as *GREEN house*). A *GREEN house* is a building, usually made of glass, in which plants are grown. However, if the word *house* is stressed (*green HOUSE*), then the sequence *green house* is not a compound but a noun phrase that is composed of the adjective *green* modifying the noun *house*. Thus, a *green HOUSE* is a house that is green.

There are other differences between noun phrases and compounds. First, the comparative *-er*, which attaches to adjectives (*richer*, *smaller*, etc.), can attach to *green* in the noun phrase *green HOUSE* to yield *greener house*. The compound interpretation is not possible in this case. Second, in the case of the noun phrase *green HOUSE* additional adjectives may be conjoined with *green*. For example, someone who talks about a *green and yellow house* is still referring to a house that is (in part) green. However, the expression *and yellow* cannot interrupt the members of a compound (**GREENandyellowhouse*).

Like simple nouns, compounds can be ambiguous. In fact, a compound can acquire a second or third meaning through the creative use of language. For example, *egg roll* can be used to refer either to a certain kind of Chinese food or to an activity that takes place (e.g., at the White House) around Easter.

Humor often taps heretofore unthought-of ambiguities. For each pair of drawings, you are to determine (1) whether the combination of words under the drawing is an ambiguous compound (a compound that is associated with two different meanings, like the example *egg roll*) or (2) whether the combination of words can be understood *either* as a compound *or* as a noun phrase (like the example *green HOUSE/GREEN house*). Study the drawings and answer questions A, B, and (optionally) C.

1. Big-Wig

2. Fish-Tank

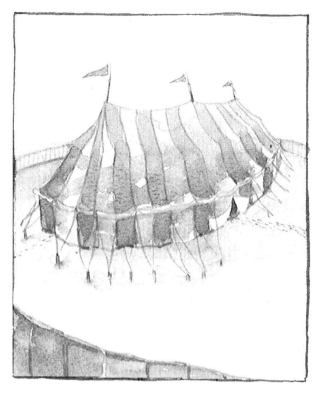

3. Big-Top

4. Cat-Food

5. White-Fish

6. Church-Key

7. Mouse-Trap

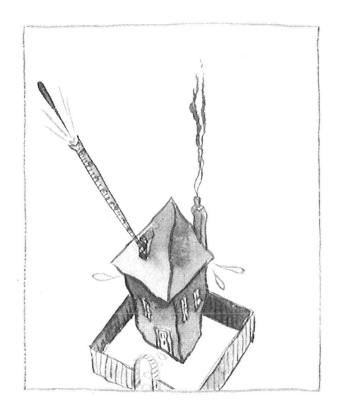

8. Hot-House

A. Which combinations of two words are ambiguous compound nouns? (List them by number.)

B. Which combinations of two words could be either a noun phrase or a compound noun? (List them by number.)

C. (*Optional*) Either draw or describe a drawing or situation similar to the pairs found in this exercise. That is, find a case of (1) a compound that has two possible meanings or (2) a case of a sequence of words that are interpretable either as a compound or as a noun phrase.

Name _____

Section _____

1.4 Word Building 1: -ness Affixation (English)

For this exercise, consider the following words:

	List I	List II
1.	furious	furiousness
2.	infectious	infectiousness
3.	courteous	courteousness
4.	powerless	powerlessness
5.	fair	fairness
6.	clever	cleverness
7.	warm	warmness
8.	useful	usefulness
9.	prideful	pridefulness
10.	heavy	heaviness
11.	slack	slackness
12.	sick	sickness
13.	sleepy	sleepiness

Questions

State the word formation rule for the affix *-ness*, using the following format (see *Linguistics*, pp. 35–40):

A. Phonological change

B. Category change
   1. What part of speech does *-ness* attach to? That is, what is the part of speech of the words in list I?

2. What is the part of speech of the derived word? That is, what is the part of speech of the words in list II?

C. Semantic change
What meaning change is caused by the suffix *-ness*? That is, in the ideal case, what element of meaning does it contribute?

1.5 Word Building 2: -like Affixation (English)

Examine the data in lists I and II and answer questions A–F. It will be helpful to review the material in *Linguistics* on parts of speech (pp. 19–23).

List I	List II
1. war	warlike
2. wife	wifelike
3. king	kinglike
4. prince	princelike
5. human	humanlike
6. snake	snakelike
7. child	childlike
8. lady	ladylike
9. tree	treelike
10. death	deathlike
11. thumb	thumblike
12. book	booklike
13. sportsman	sportsmanlike
14. dungeon	dungeonlike
15. fish	fishlike

Questions

A. The morpheme *like* combines with a word of what category (part of speech)? That is, what category is *X* in *X-like*?

B. The words in list II all belong to what category?

C. What meaning change appears to be caused by *like*? That is, in the ideal case, what element of meaning does it contribute?

D. Have any of the examples in list II *drifted* in meaning? (See *Linguistics*, pp. 49–50.) If so, which ones? In each case, how does the drifted meaning differ from the compositional meaning (i.e., the sum of the meaning of the stem, *X*, plus the meaning of *like*)?

E. Consider the following examples and answer the questions below:

idealike
justicelike
happinesslike

Can *like* combine with *any* word belonging to the category in your answer to question A? That is, can *any* word belonging to the same category as the words in list I combine with *like*? If there are restrictions, what do they appear to be?

F. Does *like* combine *only* with words of the category exemplified in list I, or can it combine with words from other categories as well? Give examples and explain.

1.6 Word Building 3: Tohono O'odham

Consider the following data from Tohono O'odham, a Native American language belonging to the Uto-Aztecan family, and answer questions A–C.

The symbol ' stands for a consonant known as a glottal stop. (A glottal stop is found at the beginning of the two *oh*'s in the English expression *oh-oh*. The glottal stop between the two *oh*'s is the easier to hear and even feel.) The symbol : indicates that the vowel preceding it is long (hence, *o:* is a long *o*). The symbol *ñ* is pronounced like the Spanish *ñ* or the English sequence *ny* in *canyon*. The symbol ˘ indicates that a vowel is short (hence, *ĭ* is short). A dot under a consonant indicates a special pronunciation with the tongue slightly curled back. The orthographic symbols are those now employed by the Tohono O'odham people. For a discussion of the phonetic value of the orthographic symbol *e*, see exercise 3.3.

	List I		List II	
	Tohono O'odham form	English gloss	Tohono O'odham form	English gloss
1.	je'e	"mother"	ñje'e	"my mother"
2.	'o:gĭ	"father"	m'o:gĭ	"your father"
3.	kakkio	"legs"	hakakkio	"their legs"
4.	no:nowĭ	"hands"	'emno:nowĭ	"your (pl.) hands"
5.	'o'ohana	"books"	t'o'ohana	"our books"
6.	kotoñ	"shirt"	kotoñij	"his/her shirt"
7.	wopnam	"hats"	twopnam	"our hats"
8.	mamgina	"cars"	'emmamgina	"your (pl.) cars"
9.	papla	"shovels"	hapapla	"their shovels"
10.	hoa	"basket"	ñhoa	"my basket"
11.	taḍ	"foot"	taḍij	"his/her foot"
12.	ki:	"house"	mki:	"your house"
13.	na:nk	"ears"	'emna:nk	"your (pl.) ears"
14.	to:ton	"knees"	hato:ton	"their knees"
15.	we:nag	"sibling"	we:nagij	"his/her sibling"
16.	si:l	"saddle"	ñsi:l	"my saddle"
17.	taḍ	"foot"	mtaḍ	"your foot"
18.	mo:mĭ	"heads"	tmo:mĭ	"our heads"
19.	na:nk	"ears"	na:nkij	"his/her ears"
20.	kakkio	"legs"	'emkakkio	"your (pl.) legs"
21.	wuhi	"eye"	ñwuhi	"my eye"
22.	mamgina	"cars"	tmamgina	"our cars"
23.	da:k	"nose"	ñda:k	"my nose"
24.	da:k	"nose"	da:kij	"his/her nose"

A. For each of the following possessive words of English, list the corresponding possessive morpheme in Tohono O'odham.

1. Possessive morpheme

   Tohono O'odham morpheme   English gloss

   a. _____   "my"

   b. _____   "your"

   c. _____   "his/her"

   d. _____   "our"

   e. _____   "your (pl.)"

   f. _____   "their"

B. The Tohono O'odham possessive morphemes are bound morphemes. Are they prefixes or suffixes?

C. What is special about the third person singular possessive morpheme (meaning "his/her") in Tohono O'odham?

1.7 Word Building 4: Tohono O'odham

Consider the following verb forms from Tohono O'odham and answer questions A and B. (The special symbols used in writing these Tohono O'odham forms are explained in exercise 1.6.)

Tohono O'odham form	English gloss
Singular	
1. ñeok	"speaks"
2. him	"walks"
3. dagkon	"wipes"
4. helwuin	"is sliding"
5. 'ul	"sticks out"
Plural	
1. ñeñeok	"we/you/they speak"
2. hihim	"we/you/they walk"
3. dadagkon	"we/you/they wipe"
4. hehelwuin	"we/you/they are sliding"
5. 'u'ul	"we/you/they stick out"

Questions

A. Describe, as precisely as you can, how the plural verbs are formed from the singular verbs. (What must be done to a singular form in order to convert it into a plural form?)

B. What is the name of the morphological process illustrated in the data? (Review the discussion of grammatical categories in *Linguistics*, pp. 19–22.)

1.8 Morphophonology 1: -ščik Affixation (Russian)

Below are two lists of Russian words. The words in list II are derived from those in list I. After studying the lists, answer questions A–D.

The two symbols *šč* (IPA: *ʃtʃ*) stand for the one letter щ in written Russian. The apostrophe (') after consonants indicates that the preceding consonant is palatalized. This phonetic feature does not play a role in the answer to this exercise, however.

The *-o* suffix on *derevo* indicates that it is a neuter noun; the *-a* suffix on *gazeta* indicates that it is a feminine noun. Ignore these suffixes for the purposes of this exercise and assume that the suffix under study attaches to the stems *derev-* and *gazet-*.

	List I		List II	
	Russian word	English gloss	Russian word	English gloss
1.	atom	"atom"	atomščik	"atomic-warmonger"
2.	baraban	"drum"	barabanščik	"drummer"
3.	kalambur	"pun"	kalamburščik	"punner"
4.	pulemyot	"machine-gun"	pulemyotčik	"machine-gunner"
5.	mebel'	"furniture"	mebel'ščik	"furniture maker"
6.	beton	"concrete"	betonščik	"concrete worker"
7.	lom	"scrap"	lomščik	"salvage collector"
8.	derevo	"tree"	derevščik	"craftsman"
9.	gazeta	"newspaper"	gazetčik	"newspaper seller" or "journalist"
10.	lyot	"flight"	lyotčik	"flier" or "pilot"

Words 1–6 are from Townsend 1975, 174.

Questions

A. The suffix that attaches to the words in list I to form the words in list II has two forms. What are they?

B. Given examples 1–10, suggest a possible reason why one form of the suffix occurs rather than the other. (Hint: Compare the ending of the stems of examples 4, 9, and 10 with the ending of the stems of all the other examples.)

C. The suffix attaches to a noun to create a noun with a new meaning. How is the meaning of the derived word related to the meaning of the basic word in list I? (Obviously, unless you know Russian, you will have to base your hypothesis on the English glosses.)

D. Given the base *apparat-*, what would you predict to be the derived Russian word that results from the rule discussed above?

1.9 Morphophonology 2: Turkish

Study the Turkish expressions below and answer questions A–C.

	Turkish form	English gloss
1.	el	"the hand"
2.	eller	"hands"
3.	elim	"my hand"
4.	ev	"the house"
5.	eve	"to the house"
6.	ellerimiz	"our hands"
7.	ellerimde	"in my hands"
8.	evlerde	"in the houses"
9.	evden	"from the house"
10.	ellerim	"my hands"
11.	ellerinize	"to your (pl.) hands"
12.	evlerim	"my houses"
13.	elin	"your (sg.) hand"
14.	evimiz	"our house"
15.	evde	"in the house"
16.	elimde	"in my hand"
17.	evlerimiz	"our houses"
18.	evlerimden	"from my houses"
19.	evleriniz	"your (pl.) houses"
20.	evim	"my house"
21.	ellerimden	"from my hands"
22.	evler	"houses"
23.	eline	"to your (sg.) hand"
24.	ellerin	"your (sg.) hands"
25.	elimden	"from my hand"
26.	evine	"to your (sg.) house"

In the English translations, *your* is listed as singular (*sg.*) when it refers to one person and as plural (*pl.*) when it refers to more than one person.

A. In the spaces below, list the Turkish morphemes that correspond to the English words on the right.

	Turkish morpheme	English gloss
1.	_____	"(the) hand"
2.	_____	"(the) house"
3.	_____	plural
4.	_____	"my"
5.	_____	"our"
6.	_____	"your (sg.)"
7.	_____	"your (pl.)"
8.	_____	"to"
9.	_____	"in"
10.	_____	"from"

B. Given the Turkish data, what is the order of the morphemes (indicating possession, person, etc.) of the suffixes in a word?

C. Based on your answers in questions A and B, how would you translate the following English forms into Turkish?

1. from your house   _____

2. to our house   _____

3. in my house   _____

Name _____

Section _____

1.10 Morphophonology 3: -ity Affixation (English)

When an affix is attached to a stem (or word) to create a new word, a nontrivial phonological change may occur (see *Linguistics*, pp. 36–37). Lists I and II illustrate just such a case. Consider the two lists of words and the relation between them, and answer the questions that follow.

List I	List II
1. eccentric	eccentricity
2. elastic	elasticity
3. opaque	opacity
4. electric	electricity
5. peptic	pepticity
6. specific	specificity
7. periodic	periodicity
8. endemic	endemicity
9. volcanic	volcanicity
10. centric	centricity
11. egocentric	egocentricity

Questions

A. Transcribe the pairs of words in lists I and II in the spaces provided. Indicate the placement of main stress (e.g., *capable* /kéɪpəbl̩/).

1. _____   _____

2. _____   _____

3. _____   _____

4. _____   _____

5. _____   _____

6. _____   _____

7. _____   _____

8. _____   _____

9. _____   _____

10. _____   _____

11. _____   _____

B. Describe what changes occur in the words in list I when the affix *-ity* is attached.

C. You may not be familiar with some of the words in the lists. However, you should have had no trouble determining where the main stress of the derived words (those in list II) is located. State a generalization about the position of the main stress in the words in list II.

2 Phonetics

2.1 Reverse Transcription

Question

The following is an untitled poem by James Joyce (1946). In the spaces provided between the lines, write a reverse transcription (convert to the standard English orthography). Each word has been written as if it were produced in isolation, an idealization that simplifies the reverse transcription task. The vowels in each pair ʌ-ə and ɝ-ɚ are very similar in pronunciation; the former pair sounds like the vowel in *butt*, the latter pair like the vowel in *Burt*. For a discussion of why two different symbols are used to transcribe each of these pairs, see *Linguistics*, pp. 126–140 (esp. p. 138).

1. ðʌ twaɪlaɪt tɝnz fɹʌm æməθɪst

2. tu dip ænd dipɚ blu.

3. ðʌ læmp fɪlz wɪθ ʌ peɪl gɹin glou

4. ðʌ tɹiz ʌv ðʌ ævənu.

5. ðʌ ould piænou pleɪz æn ɛɹ,

6. sədeɪt ænd slou ænd geɪ.

7. ʃi bɛnz əpɑn ðʌ jɛlou kiz,

8. hɝ hɛd ɪnklaɪnz ðɪs weɪ.

9. ʃaɪ θɑts* ænd gɹeɪv waɪd aɪz ænd hænz

10. ðæt wɑndɚ æz ðeɪ lɪst—

11. ðʌ twaɪlaɪt tɝnz tu dɑɹkɚ blu

12. wɪθ laɪts ʌv æməθɪst.

*(or *θɔts*, depending on the dialect)

Name _____

Section _____

2.2 Transcription: Monosyllables

Question

Write the following monosyllabic words using the transcription system given in appendix 3. Be sure not to be fooled by the orthography.

1. fish _____	16. plan _____	31. laugh _____
2. thin _____	17. pooch _____	32. rough _____
3. then _____	18. pouch _____	33. thought _____
4. hitch _____	19. peach _____	34. drought _____
5. ping _____	20. rouge _____	35. though _____
6. taste _____	21. dew _____	36. cog _____
7. sheep _____	22. do _____	37. clinch _____
8. try _____	23. due _____	38. raw _____
9. live _____	24. fin _____	39. lawn _____
10. life _____	25. vine _____	40. gone _____
11. jut _____	26. roof _____	41. lath _____
12. Goth _____	27. bang _____	42. lathe _____
13. juke _____	28. dung _____	43. soot _____
14. hoof _____	29. with _____	44. crush _____
15. hooves _____	30. width _____	45. ought _____

2.3 Phonetic Variation: Spanish /b/, /d/, /g/

Below is a broad transcription of some Spanish words. [b]/[β], [d]/[ð], and [g]/[ɣ] are pairs of allophones whose members are in complementary distribution; that is, they occur in mutually exclusive (or nonoverlapping) phonetic environments. (See *Linguistics*, pp. 93–97.)

[β] is a voiced bilabial fricative.
[ð] is a voiced interdental fricative.
[ɣ] is a voiced dorsovelar fricative.

	Spanish form	English gloss		Spanish form	English gloss
1.	[aɣrio]	"sour"	14.	[kaβe]	"it fits"
2.	[gustar]	"to please"	15.	[eðað]	"age"
3.	[xweɣo]	"game"	16.	[komuniðað]	"community"
4.	[albondiɣas]	"meatballs"	17.	[deðo]	"finger/toe"
5.	[gastos]	"expenses"	18.	[droɣas]	"drugs"
6.	[gonsales]	surname	19.	[seða]	"silk"
7.	[ɣaɣa]	"sore, boil"	20.	[ganaðo]	"cattle"
8.	[uβa]	"grape"	21.	[usteð]	"you (sg. polite)"
9.	[futbol]	"soccer"	22.	[bastante]	"plenty"
10.	[kaldo]	"broth"	23.	[brinkar]	"to jump"
11.	[algo]	"something"	24.	[suβo]	"I climb"
12.	[sombra]	"shade"	25.	[uβo]	"there was"
13.	[saβino]	"cypress"	26.	[kluβ]	"club"

Questions

A. When do the voiced stops [b], [d], and [g] occur?

B. When do the voiced fricatives [β], [ð], and [ɣ] occur?

C. Given the distribution of the voiced stops versus the voiced fricatives described in your answers to questions A and B, decide which sounds ([b], [d], [g] *or* [β], [ð], [ɣ]) are basic and which are derived.

2.4 Special Topic 1: Phonetic Variation (English /t/)

The phoneme /t/ in English has six allophones, whose conditioning environments are summarized in the following table. (See *Linguistics*, pp. 90–93.) After examining the table, answer questions A and B.

Articulatory description	Phonetic symbol	Conditioning environment	Example words
Released, aspirated	[tʰ]	when syllable-initial	tin [tʰɪn]
Unreleased, preglottalized	[ˀt]	word-final, after a vowel	kit [kʰɪˀt]
Glottal stop	[ʔ]	before a syllabic *n*	kitten [kʰɪʔn̩]
Flap	[ɾ]	between vowels, when the first vowel is stressed (approximate environment)	pitted [pʰíɾɨd]
Alveopalatal stop	[t̪]	syllable-initial before *r*	truck [t̪ɹ̥ʌk]
Released, unaspirated	[t]	when the above conditions are not met first	stint [stɪnt]

Questions

A. Identify the variant of /t/ in each word below. For some dialects of English the "conditioning environments" described in the table are not descriptively adequate and require modification. Check to see if in your dialect any adjustments need to be made in the environments.

Word	Variant of /t/	Conditioning environment
1. after	_____	_____
2. beautiful	_____	_____
3. embitter	_____	_____

4. that   _____   _____

5. cotton   _____   _____

6. cent   _____   _____

7. Burt   _____   _____

8. built   _____   _____

9. butler   _____   _____

10. Burton   _____   _____

11. substance   _____   _____

12. atoms   _____   _____

13. result   _____   _____

14. phonetics   _____   _____

15. revolt   _____   _____

16. antler   _____   _____

17. settler   _____   _____

18. try   _____   _____

19. attitude   _____   _____

20. article   _____   _____

B. In the spaces provided, write your rules for changing /t/ to [tʰ], [ʔt], [ʔ], [ɾ], [t̪], and [t], respectively. You may want to refer to appendix 1 for instructions on how to write phonological rules.

1.

2.

3.

4.

5.

6.

2.5 Special Topic 2: Transcription (Vowels before /ɹ/)

Questions

Write the following words containing the phoneme /ɹ/, using the transcription system given in appendix 3 and in *Linguistics* (review pp. 97–100).

A. 1. boor _____ 6. dear _____

    2. bore _____ 7. fir _____

    3. poor _____ 8. mire _____

    4. care _____ 9. sewer _____

    5. car _____ 10. mirror _____

B. 1. tier _____ 6. lawyer _____

    2. Bayer _____ 7. earn _____

    3. merry _____ 8. lower _____

    4. marry _____ 9. sour _____

    5. Mary _____ 10. seer _____

Name _____

Section _____

2.6 Writing Systems: Japanese

The Japanese language can be written in several different ways. One method (*kanji*) is based on characters borrowed from the Chinese writing system. Another (*romaji*) uses letters from the roman alphabet; this system is used to write the Japanese in this workbook. Yet another writing system, the *katakana* syllabary, uses symbols that represent consonant-plus-vowel sequences (refer to *Linguistics*, pp. 563–567, for information on syllable-based writing systems). The chart below is a partial list of the symbols that make up the katakana syllabary of Japanese. Study the symbols and their pronunciations, and answer questions A–E.

1. カ /ka/   キ /ki/   ク /ku/   ケ /ke/   コ /ko/
2. サ /sa/   シ /ši/   ス /su/   セ /se/   ソ /so/
3. タ /ta/   チ /či/   ツ /tsu/   テ /te/   ト /to/
4. ナ /na/   ニ /ni/   ヌ /nu/   ネ /ne/   ノ /no/
5. ハ /ha/   ヒ /hi/   フ /fu/   ヘ /he/   ホ /ho/
6. マ /ma/   ミ /mi/   ム /mu/   メ /me/   モ /mo/

Questions

A. Consider the following examples:

1. ガ /ga/
2. ギ /gi/
3. グ /gu/
4. ゴ /go/

What important role does the diacritic ` play?

B. Based on your answer to question A, transcribe these symbols:

1. ザ /   /
2. デ /   /
3. ゼ /   /
4. ド /   /

C. Would it make sense for the diacritic ゛ to be added to any of the following symbols: ニ, ノ, マ, ム? Why or why not?

D. The diacritic ゛ indicates a voiced bilabial stop when associated with the symbols in line 5. Transcribe the following symbols. For example: バ /ba/.

1. ビ /   /
2. ブ /   /
3. ベ /   /
4. ボ /   /

E. The diacritic ° is combined with the katakana symbols in one of the above lines to indicate /pa/, /pi/, /pu/, /pe/, or /po/.

1. Write the katakana symbols that represent the following sound combinations. (The symbol ° should be written to the upper right of the basic symbols you have chosen.)

    a. _____ /pa/

    b. _____ /pi/

    c. _____ /pu/

    d. _____ /pe/

    e. _____ /po/

2. Why did you choose the symbols you did?

3. What does the diacritic ° represent?

3 Phonology

Name _____

Section _____

3.1 Phonological Rules 1: English Past Tense

The examples in list I are representative of English verbs that form a regular past tense (i.e., their past tense form can be predicted). These past tense forms are shown in list II. Like the English plural morpheme, the English regular past tense morpheme has three variants: in this case, [t], [d], and [ɪd].

Consider the data in lists I and II. (To facilitate your study, write the last sound of each word in the space provided.) Answer questions A–F, referring to distinctive features in your answers. (Instructions on writing rules are found in appendixes 1 and 2, and a list of distinctive features is found in appendix 4.)

List I	Last sound of verb	List II	[t], [d], or [ɪd]
1. please	[z]	pleased	[d]
2. grab	_____	grabbed	_____
3. slam	_____	slammed	_____
4. plan	_____	planned	_____
5. fit	_____	fitted	_____
6. fix	_____	fixed	_____
7. pack	_____	packed	_____
8. peep	_____	peeped	_____
9. blend	_____	blended	_____
10. seethe	_____	seethed	_____
11. bomb	_____	bombed	_____
12. hang	_____	hanged	_____
13. fog	_____	fogged	_____
14. flush	_____	flushed	_____
15. knit	_____	knitted	_____
16. fade	_____	faded	_____

Questions

A. In what environment does [t] occur? List the relevant segments and provide the distinctive features these segments have in common.

B. In what environment does [d] occur? List the relevant segments and provide the distinctive features these segments have in common.

C. In what environment does [ɨd] occur? List the relevant segments and provide the distinctive features these segments have in common.

D. What does the distribution (pattern of occurrence) of the past tense morpheme [t] have in common with the distribution of the plural morpheme [s]?

E. What does the distribution of past tense [d] have in common with the distribution of plural [z]?

F. What does the distribution of past tense [ɨd] have in common with the distribution of plural [ɨz]?

3.2 Phonological Rules 2: Korean [l] and [r]

In Korean the sounds [l] and [r] are in complementary distribution. Examine the data below and answer the questions that follow.

		Korean word	English gloss
A.	1.	pal	"foot"
		paruy	"of the foot"
	2.	mul	"water"
		muruy	"of the water"
	3.	ssal	"rice"
		ssaruy	"of the rice"
	4.	saram	"person"
		saramuy	"of the person"
B.	5.	sul	"liquor"
		sultok	"liquor jug"
	6.	mul	"water"
		multok	"water jug"
	7.	ssal	"rice"
		ssaltok	"rice jug"
C.	8.	khal	"knife"
	9.	səul	"Seoul"
	10.	ilkop	"seven"
	11.	ipalsa	"barber"
	12.	məri	"head, hair"
	13.	rupi	"ruby"
	14.	ratio	"radio"

The data in 9–11 and 13–14 are from Fromkin and Rodman 1988, 116. There are two s's in Korean, one transcribed here as s (lax) and the other as ss (fortis).

A. Given the data in set A (1–4), what is the form of the affix meaning "of (the)"?

B. What happens to [l] when the affix meaning "of (the)" is attached to the stem?

C. Given the data in set B (5–7), what is the form of the morpheme meaning "vessel for holding X" (glossed here as "jug")?

D. Considering both sets of data, A (1–4) and B (5–7), what generalizations can you make regarding the distribution of [l] and [r]? That is, where does [r] occur and where does [l] occur?

E. 1. Assume for the moment that [l] is basic. What would be the phonological rule necessary to derive [r]? (That is, $l \rightarrow r/\ldots?\ldots$)

2. Assume for the moment that [r] is basic. What would be the phonological rule necessary to derive [l]? (That is, r → l/...?...)

3. Which rule, E-1 or E-2, would be preferable? That is, which rule is simpler, the rule deriving [l] from [r] or the rule deriving [r] from [l]?

F. Now consider the monomorphemic Korean words in set C (8–14). Does the generalization that you stated in question D hold true for these examples as well? If not, modify the rule you chose in question E-3 so that it accounts for these examples.

G. Is the phonological rule that you chose in question E-3 compatible with the generalization that you found in question F? If not, modify your rule so that it is.

H. Assuming the phonological rule that you developed in questions E–G, provide the underlying or basic representation of the words for "knife," "seven," and "ruby."

3.3 Phonological Rules 3: Tohono O'odham

In Tohono O'odham, a Native American language belonging to the Uto-Aztecan family, the sounds *ḍ* and *ṣ* are variants of the sounds *r* and *s*, respectively. That is, *r* and *s* are basic and *ḍ* and *ṣ* are derived. The *ḍ* is a voiced retroflex stop consonant, and the *ṣ* is a voiceless retroflex fricative. The complete list of Tohono O'odham speech sounds contains /p, t, k, ʔ, b, d, ḍ, g, h, ǰ, l, m, ñ, n, r, s, ṣ, w (v), y, č, a, ɨ, i, o, u, a:, ɨ:, i:, o:, u:/. The phonetic symbol *ɨ* is a high back unrounded vowel. The Tohono O'odham use the symbol *e* to write this sound since the Tohono O'odham language does not have a mid front vowel (English /eɪ/ and /ɛ/).

Examine the Tohono O'odham forms listed below and answer questions A–C. Instructions for writing phonological rules are found in appendixes 1 and 2.

	Tohono O'odham form	English gloss
1.	ʔaridt	"had a baby"
2.	ṣo:m	"sew"
3.	kuḍut	"bother"
4.	ṣɨ:piǰ	"younger brother, cousin"
5.	taḍaǰ	"his/her/its foot"
6.	ʔarik	"to be a baby"
7.	ʔɨḍapi	"gut, remove entrails"
8.	hi:kas	"cut"
9.	wuḍañ	"tie it!, rope it!"
10.	wuḍo	"untie"
11.	maṣad	"moon," "month"
12.	kuṣo	"back of neck"
13.	ṣoṣa	"mucous," "cried"
14.	si:s	"younger brother"
15.	bidk	"will be mud"
16.	wiḍut	"swing" (verb)
17.	ma:kis	"gift, something given"
18.	bisč	"sneeze"
19.	huḍuñ	"evening"
20.	kɨriw	"shuck object"
21.	mɨriñ	"run!"
22.	ṣa:d	"herd, shoo"

Questions

A. What environment conditions the occurrence of the sounds ṣ and ḍ? That is, describe the phonological environments by listing the sounds whose occurrence is associated with the derived consonants ṣ and ḍ.

B. What distinctive features uniquely describe the natural class of sounds that condition the change of s to ṣ and r to ḍ?

C. Given the rule schema A → B / C ____ D (see rule 3 in appendix 1), state the rule for the occurrence of ṣ and ḍ in Tohono O'odham. The change of s and r to ṣ and ḍ may be stated in terms of segments, as shown below; but the conditioning environment should be stated in terms of distinctive features. C and D in the schema are "placeholders" (variables). In any actual rule that conforms to the schema A → B / C ____ D, one or the other of C and D may be empty. That is, the change from s and r to ṣ and ḍ may be conditioned (1) by something that occurs before s and r *and* something that occurs after (C and D), (2) by something that occurs before s and r (C only), or (3) by something that occurs after s and r (D only).

$$\begin{bmatrix} s \\ r \end{bmatrix} \rightarrow \begin{bmatrix} ṣ \\ ḍ \end{bmatrix}$$

3.4 Phonological Rules 4: Zoque

In the following forms from Zoque, a language spoken in Mexico, many of the symbols represent consonants whose properties can be predicted from the environment in which they occur. Study the forms and answer questions A–D. Instructions for writing phonological rules are found in appendixes 1 and 2.

The complete inventory of Zoque phonemes is /p, t, t^s, t^y, č, k, s, š, h, l, ʔ, m, n, ñ, ŋ, w, x, y, i, e, ə, a, o, u/.

	Zoque form	English gloss
1.	əŋd^{y}oʔys	"he got sleepy"
2.	kenba	"he sees"
3.	nd^{z}in	"my pine"
4.	t^{y}ət^{y}əy	"little"
5.	pama	"clothing"
6.	ñǰeht^{s}u	"you cut"
7.	mingeʔtu	"he also came"
8.	mbama	"my clothing"
9.	nd^{y}uku	"you shot"
10.	ngengeʔtu	"I also saw it"
11.	petpa	"he sweeps"
12.	wixtu	"he walked"
13.	pəndaʔm	"men"
14.	myaŋdamu	"you went"
15.	nət^{y}uxu	"he's shouting"
16.	t^{s}eht^{s}u	"he cut brush"
17.	ñǰinu	"he planted it"
18.	čehčaxu	"they cut it"
19.	anǰiʔu	"goatee"
20.	čəknaʔču	"he frightened him"

A. You should be able to determine from the data that the sounds *b* and *p* are related phonologically. Given that *p* is the basic form, what is the environment that conditions the appearance of *b*? That is, list the sounds that condition the appearance of derived *b*.

B. List the distinctive feature(s) that characterize(s) the class of phonemes that condition the change of *p* to *b*.

C. You may have noticed that *p* is not the only consonant that has a variant in the environment described in question B. Identify the consonants that are subject to this rule. List the consonants that are the input to this rule on the left side of the arrow, and list the corresponding derived consonants on the right side of the arrow.

p → b

D. Write the rule for Zoque discussed in question C using the rule schema A → B / C＿＿D. Using distinctive feature notation, describe the natural class of consonants that are subject to the rule as A, indicate the feature(s) that result from the application of the rule as B, and write the conditioning environment from question B as C and D.

3.5 Phonological Rules 5: Japanese

Below are two lists of Japanese verb forms. List I consists of the base forms of verbs to which various affixes can be attached. List II consists of base forms to which the suffix -*te* has been added. This morpheme indicates continuous/progressive action, as in *Ima ame ga* *futte* *imasu* "It's raining now." Examine the data in the two lists and answer the questions that follow.

List I		List II
Japanese base form	English gloss	Japanese -*te* form
1. tabe-	"eat"	tabete
2. yob-	"call"	yonde
3. shin-	"die"	shinde
4. kak-	"write"	kaite
5. yom-	"read"	yonde
6. mi-	"see"	mite
7. asob-	"play"	asonde
8. tob-	"fly"	tonde
9. aruk-	"walk"	aruite
10. nom-	"drink"	nonde

Questions

A. For the purposes of this exercise, assume that -*te* is attached to the base forms in list I. Questions A-1 through A-4 ask you to propose phonological rules to account for the forms in list II. That is, they ask you to show how, with a small number of rules, the phonological alternations that the base forms and the suffix -*te* undergo during the suffixation process can be accounted for.

See appendix 1 for instructions on how to write informal phonological rules. The answer to question A-1 is given to illustrate the form the rules should take in this exercise.

1. Write the rule that accounts for the alternation in the forms given in example 3.

   Answer

   Rule 1: $t \rightarrow d \; / \; \begin{bmatrix} \text{voiced} \\ \text{consonantal} \end{bmatrix}$ ____

   or $t \rightarrow [+\text{voiced}]/[+\text{voiced}, +\text{consonantal}]$ ____

2. Write the rule that accounts for the alternations in examples 4 and 9.

   Rule 2:

3. To account for the list II forms in examples 5 and 10, two rules are needed, one of which has already been stated as rule 1. Write a second rule that, when applied in combination with rule 1, will produce the list II forms in examples 5 and 10. Does the order in which these rules apply make any difference?

   Rule 3:

4. Examples 2, 7, and 8 introduce yet another complication in the phonology of Japanese. They illustrate again that rules in a grammar may (or must) be ordered with respect to each other. Only one additional rule needs to be added to your list of rules if the output of this rule is allowed to "feed into" the rules you have already written. Write this rule as rule 4.

   Rule 4:

B. List the rules that are needed to derive each of the forms given in list II, ordering them where necessary. That is, list them in the order in which they must apply to derive the correct forms. Use the numbers to refer to the rules.

   1. tabete _____

   2. yonde _____

   3. shinde _____

4. kaite   _____

5. yonde   _____

6. mite   _____

7. asonde   _____

8. tonde   _____

9. aruite   _____

10. nonde   _____

C. Based on rules 1–4, what would you guess to be the -*te* form for the base *nug-*? Given the data in lists I and II, there are two possible answers. Why is this so? (Hint: *g* is like *k* in some respects, but like *d* and *b* in others.) Discuss which of the rules 1–4 may be potentially applicable (with some adjustments).

D. Can the base form of *erande* "be choosing" be predicted by rules 1–4? Why or why not?

3.6 Phonological Rules 6: Japanese

Examine the following data from Japanese and answer the questions.

Japanese form	English gloss
1. aketa	"opened"
2. akerareta	"was opened"
3. akesaseta	"caused to open"
4. akesaserareta	"was caused to open"
5. tabeta	"ate"
6. taberareta	"was eaten"
7. tabesaseta	"caused to eat"
8. tabesaserareta	"was caused to eat"
9. yonda	"read" (past)
10. yomareta	"was read"
11. yomaseta	"caused to read"
12. yomaserareta	"was caused to read"
13. tonda	"flew"
14. tobareta	"was flown"
15. tobaseta	"caused to fly"
16. tobaserareta	"was caused to fly"
17. ataeta	"awarded"
18. ataerareta	"was awarded"
19. ataesaseta	"caused to award"
20. ataesaserareta	"was caused to award"
21. eranda	"chose"
22. erabareta	"was chosen"
23. erabaseta	"caused to choose"
24. erabaserareta	"was caused to choose"

A. What are the Japanese morphemes that correspond to each of the following words in English?

	Japanese form	English gloss
1.	_____	"open"
2.	_____	"eat"
3.	_____	"read"
4.	_____	"fly"
5.	_____	"award"
6.	_____	"choose"

B. 1. The past tense suffix appears in two forms. What are they?

2. Write an informal phonological rule that changes one form of the suffix into the other. Use the correct distinctive feature(s) in stating the rule (see appendix 2). (Hint: Assume *ta* is basic.)

C. 1. The causative suffix appears in two forms. What are they?

2. What conditions determine which form of the suffix occurs?

D. 1. The passive suffix appears in two forms. What are they?

   2. What conditions determine which form of the suffix occurs?

   3. Write a phonological rule that relates the two forms of the suffix. Use the correct distinctive feature(s) in stating the rule (see appendix 2).

E. Is there any similarity between the causative and passive affixes? (Examine your responses to questions C-2 and D-2.)

F. Is there any similarity between the continuative/progressive -te form of the verb analyzed in exercise 3.5 and the past tense form?

3.7 Special Topic 1: Assigning Syllables and Feet to English Words

Question

Associate the words in A–H with syllables and metrical feet. Be sure to make use of the Maximal Onset Principle for all word-internal consonant clusters. (For a discussion of syllables and feet, see *Linguistics*, pp. 126–140.)

Word A has been supplied with syllables and feet, as a model.

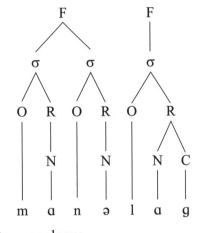

A. monologue

s i ʒ ɚ

B. seizure

t ɔ ɹ ɨ n t

C. torrent

t ɔ ɹ m ɛ n t

D. torment

ɛ l ɨ v eɪ t   ɹ i f ɝ b ɨ ʃ

E. elevate   F. refurbish

f æ n t æ s t ɨ k

G. fantastic

ɹ ʌ m p ə l s t ɪ l t s k ɨ n

H. Rumpelstiltskin

3.8 Special Topic 2: Assigning Syllables and Feet to English Words

Question

Write a phonemic transcription for words A–H and associate the phonemic transcription with syllables and metrical feet. Be sure to make use of the Maximal Onset Principle for all word-internal consonant clusters. Some of these words can be associated with different foot configurations, depending on dialect. (For a discussion of syllables and feet, see *Linguistics*, pp. 126–140.)

Word A is displayed with phonemic transcriptions and with syllables and feet, as a model.

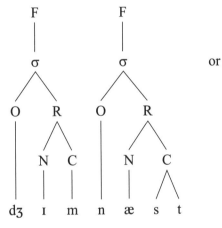 or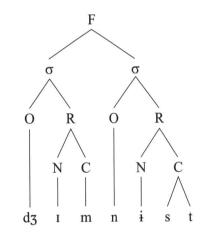

A. gymnast

B. gymnastics   C. hiatus

D. present (verb)   E. present (noun)

F. canoe   G. exacerbate

H. predatory

3.9 Special Topic 3: Phonetic Variation (French Vowels)

Examine the following data from French and answer questions A–D. (Assume that /e/ ~ /ɛ/, /ö/ ~ /ɔ̈/, and /o/ ~ /ɔ/ form three pairs of allophones.)

	French form		English gloss
1.	/bote/	beauté	"beauty"
2.	/bɛl/	belle	"beautiful"
3.	/pö/	peu	"small amount"
4.	/pɔ̈r/	peur	"fear"
5.	/mo/	mot	"word"
6.	/mɔr/	mort	"death"

Questions

A. In what environment do /e/, /ö/, and /o/ occur? (Hint: Look at syllable structure.)

B. In what environment do /ɛ/, /ɔ̈/, and /ɔ/ occur? (Hint: Again, look at syllable structure.)

C. According to the following chart, what single feature distinguishes /e/, /ö/, and /o/ from /ε/, /ȫ/, and /ɔ/?

	e	ε	ö	ȫ	o	ɔ
Back	−	−	−	−	+	+
Round	−	−	+	+	+	+
Tense	+	−	+	−	+	−

D. The word *bête* "beast" is pronounced [bεt]. What role do you think the symbol ˆ is playing here? (Hint: Note that the final orthographic *e* is not pronounced. Also, an alternative spelling in an earlier stage of French was *bette*.)

3.10 Special Topic 4: Liaison (French)

Examine the data in list I and answer question A; then consult the data in list II in order to answer questions B–E.

List I

French orthography	Pronunciation	English gloss
1. petit	[pəti]	"little"
2. vous	[vu]	"you"
3. premier	[prəmje]	"first"
4. comment	[kɔmã]	"(adv.) how"
5. nous	[nu]	"we"
6. mangez	[mãʒe]	"(you pl.) eat"

List II

French orthography	Pronunciation	English gloss
1. petit morceau	[pətimɔrso]	"little bit"
2. petit avion	[pətitavjɔ̃]	"little airplane"
3. vous avez	[vuzave]	"you have"
4. vous buvez	[vubyve]	"you are drinking"
5. premier étage	[prəmjɛretaʒ]	"first floor"
6. premier garçon	[prəmjegarsɔ̃]	"first boy"
7. comment allez-vous	[kɔmãtalevu]	"how are you (lit. going)?"
8. comment venez-vous	[kɔmãvənevu]	"how are you coming?"
9. nous avons	[nuzavɔ̃]	"we have"
10. nous buvons	[nubyvɔ̃]	"we are drinking"
11. mangez-en	[mãʒezã]	"(you pl.) eat some (of it)"
12. mangez-la (la pomme)	[mãʒela]	"(you pl.) eat it (the apple)"

A. Compare the orthographic representations in list I with the phonetic representations ("Pronunciation" column); ignore the vowels. How do the phonetic representations consistently differ from the orthographic ones?

B. How do the data in list I differ from the data in list II?

C. Describe what appears to be conditioning the change(s) that you noted in question B.

D. On the basis of your hypothesis in question C, provide the *underlying* representations for the words in list I (i.e., the phonemic representation indicated by /   /). (See *Linguistics*, pp. 121–124.)

1. petit   _____

2. vous   _____

3. premier   _____

4. comment   _____

5. nous   _____

6. mangez   _____

E. Provide evidence to support your answer in question D.

4 Syntax

4.1 English Syntax 1: Simple Phrase Structure Rules

Consider the following two sets of phrase structure rules for English, and answer questions A–D. You may find it helpful to review *Linguistics*, pp. 201–206.

Phrase structure rules

Set I   Set II

1. S → NP Aux VP   1. S → NP Aux VP
2. NP → Art N PP   2. NP → Art N
3. PP → P NP   3. VP → V NP PP
4. VP → V NP   4. NP → Art N
5. NP → Art N PP   5. PP → P NP
6. PP → P NP   6. NP → Art N
7. NP → Art N

Questions

A. Draw the phrase structure tree that is defined by applying the phrase structure rules 1–7 in set I. Be sure to apply the rules in the order they are given. (In other words, apply rule 1; then apply rule 2 to the output of rule 1; and so forth.)

B. Give an appropriate sentence for the tree you have drawn in question A.

C. Draw the phrase structure tree that is defined by applying the phrase structure rules 1–6 in set II, in the order they are given.

D. Give an appropriate sentence for the tree you have drawn in question C.

4.2 English Syntax 2: Simple NPs, VPs, and PPs

Provide the following tree structures. To do so, you may find it helpful to review *Linguistics*, pp. 201–206.

Questions

A. Draw a tree structure for each of the following noun phrases:

1. the boy in the tree

2. a sign on the door

B. Draw a tree structure for each of the following verb phrases:

1. hit the ball

2. hammered the nail into the wall

C. Draw a tree structure for each of the following prepositional phrases:

1. up the tree in the yard

2. on the desk near the window

D. Draw a tree structure for each of the following sentences:

1. The boy in the tree near the house threw the ball into the yard.

2. The professor put the book about linguistics on the table near the podium.

4.3 English Syntax 3: Ill-Formed Trees

The tree structures 1–8 are all ill formed. That is, there is no combination of phrase structure rules or transformations that will generate any of them. Study the trees and answer the question.

1.
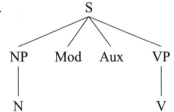

2.
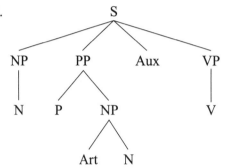

3.
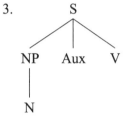

4.
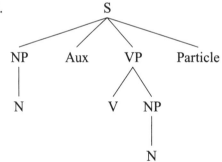

5.
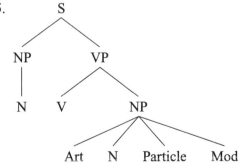

6.
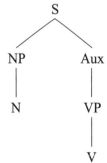

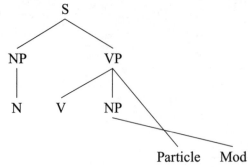

7. ... 8. ...

(tree diagrams labeled 7 and 8)

Question

For each tree, state what the problem is (i.e., why it cannot be generated by the phrase structure rules) and correct it when possible *without* altering the linear order of any of the nodes. A list of some of the phrase structure rules for English is given in appendix 5. You may find it helpful to review *Linguistics*, pp. 201–206.

1.

2.

3.

4.

5.

6.

7.

8.

4.4 English Syntax 4: Tree and Sentence Matching

Below are three sentences and four structures. Match each structure with a
sentence and then answer questions A–E.

1. [The doctor] called the patient up on the phone.
2. [John saw] a girl with a telescope.
3. [The boy's father,] who works at IBM, plays chess.

Structure I

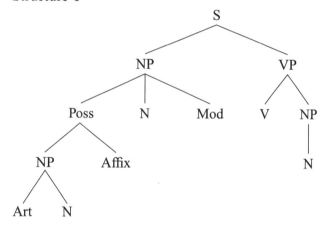

Structure II

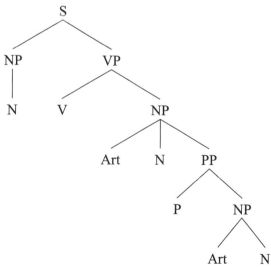

Structure III

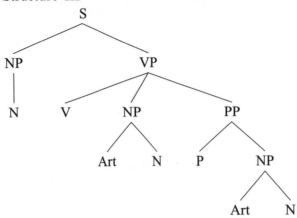

Structure IV

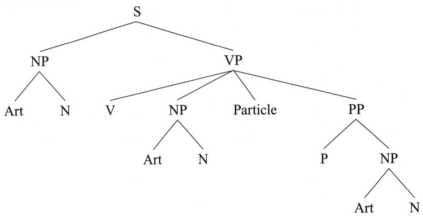

Questions

A. Why can three sentences be associated with four structures in the above examples? That is, why are the sentences 1, 2, and 3 associated with four structures?

B. One of the sentences is the output of a transformation discussed in chapter 5 of *Linguistics*. Which sentence is it? (Hint: Review *Linguistics*, pp. 183–197.)

C. Which transformation is involved in generating the sentence that is your answer to question B?

D. What is the input sentence for the transformation mentioned in question C?

E. What is the tree structure for the sentence you have written in answer to question D? That is, what is the input tree for the transformation mentioned in question C?

Name _____

Section _____

4.5 English Syntax 5: Possessive NP with a PP

In this exercise you will be asked to draw the tree structure for the following sentence:

The baby on the doctor's lap's mother will visit her brother.

Considering the following questions first will help you in determining the correct tree structure. It will also be helpful to review *Linguistics*, pp. 209–211.

1. Who will "visit her brother"?
2. What would be an appropriate tag question for the sentence? (On tag questions, see *Linguistics*, pp. 161–164, 169.)
3. Whose mother is it?
4. Where is the baby?
5. What phrase structure rules will be required to generate the subject constituent of the sentence? To answer this question, look for items like prepositions, articles, and possessive affixes.

Question

Provide the tree structure for the example sentence.

4.6 English Syntax 6: Verb-Particle versus Verb-PP Structure

Each of the sentences 1–6 involves either a verb + particle followed by a noun phrase (structure I) or a verb followed by a prepositional phrase (structure II).

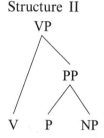

Structure I

Structure II

1. John ran into the street.
2. Paul called up Tim.
3. The child slipped into the closet.
4. I calmed down the clerk.
5. The student filled in the blanks.
6. Deer can leap over the fence.

Below you will be asked to determine which of the two structures is relevant for each sentence. To make this determination, use the following constituent structure tests:

Cleft construction (see *Linguistics*, pp. 178–179)

It is/was *X* that *Y*.

A single constituent substitutes for *X* in this construction. For example, consider the sentence *Sally threw out the garbage*. Assume that *out the garbage* is a single constituent (i.e., an instance of structure II). If this assumption is correct, then *out the garbage* should be able to substitute for *X* in the cleft construction to produce a grammatical sentence. However, **It was out the garbage that Sally threw* is not a grammatical sentence, indicating that *out the garbage* is not a single constituent and consequently that the VP structure for *threw out the garbage* is I, not II.

Conjunction (see *Linguistics*, pp. 179–181)

X and *Y*

X and *Y* must be of the same category (as for instance in *He threw the pen* [PP *through the window*] *and* [PP *onto the floor*]). For example, if *out the garbage* is a PP in *Sally threw out the garbage*, then it should be possible to conjoin another PP—say, *into the can*—with it. But the resulting sentence is ungrammatical: **Sally threw out the garbage and into the can*. Conclusion: *out the garbage* is not a PP. The relevant structure for the VP is again shown to be I, not II.

Particle Movement transformation (see *Linguistics*, pp. 198–201)

SD: X – V – Particle – NP – Y
     1   2   3   4   5 ⟹
SC: 1   2   ∅   4 + 3 5
          (or: V NP + Particle)

If the cleft and conjunction tests have failed to yield a grammatical sentence, then this predicts that the sentence in question involves an instance of the verb + particle construction (structure I) and that the Particle Movement transformation should be able to apply. In our example, applying Particle Movement to *Sally threw out the garbage* indeed produces a grammatical sentence (*Sally threw the garbage out*), indicating again that *threw out the garbage* is an instance of structure I.

Questions

Apply the three constituent structure tests to sentences 1–6 to determine which structure (I or II) is correct for each one. In the spaces provided, state which structure is correct for each sentence and give the evidence for your answer (i.e., mention the results of the tests).

1.

    Cleft:

    Conjunction:

    Particle Movement:

2.

    Cleft:

    Conjunction:

    Particle Movement:

3.

   Cleft:

   Conjunction:

   Particle Movement:

4.

   Cleft:

   Conjunction:

   Particle Movement:

5.

   Cleft:

   Conjunction:

   Particle Movement:

6.

   Cleft:

   Conjunction:

   Particle Movement:

Below are more examples (7–12) for extra practice.

7. The athlete worked out the problem.
8. She washed off her shoes.
9. The lady fell down the stairs.
10. She let down her hair.
11. He helped out the child.
12. He walked out the door.

4.7 English Syntax 7: S-Adverbs versus VP-Adverbs

In chapter 5 of *Linguistics* a distinction is made between S-adverbs and VP-adverbs (see pp. 199–201). S-adverbs have scope over (i.e., modify) the entire sentence; VP-adverbs have scope over (i.e., modify) just the VP. A test for determining whether an adverb is an S-adverb or a VP-adverb is whether it can occur in the *X* position in

It is/was *X* the case that *Y*.

If it can, then it is an S-adverb. For example, *surely*, which is an S-adverb, can substitute for *X* (*It is surely the case that Paula will succeed*), whereas *quickly*, which is not an S-adverb, cannot (**It is quickly the case that Paula will succeed*).
   Consider the following examples and answer questions A–D.

1a. John listened to the music *intently*.
 b. John listened to the music *finally*.

2a. Mary speaks French *fluently*.
 b. Mary speaks French *happily*.

3a. Paul taunted her *unfortunately*.
 b. Paul taunted her *unjustly*.

Questions

A. Which adverbs are S-adverbs? Provide evidence to support your decisions (i.e., provide the relevant example sentences). (Caution: Be sure that the sense of the original sentence has not been altered in the "test" sentence.)

B. Which adverbs are VP-adverbs? Provide evidence to support your decisions.

C. At least one adverb is ambiguous with respect to its status (i.e., it can be either an S-adverb or a VP-adverb). Which adverb(s) do you consider ambiguous and why?

D. Determine the status of the following adverbs (i.e., whether each one is an S-adverb or a VP-adverb), providing relevant example sentences to support your decisions.

1. fortunately

2. forcibly

3. openly

4. certainly

4.8 English Syntax 8: Arguing for Syntactic Structure

Consider the following sentence and answer the questions below:

The TA who is entering the room will pass out the exam at the door.

Questions

A. Draw a tree structure for the example sentence given above.

B. Determine five pieces of evidence that support the structure you have drawn in question A. For example, you can use the following constructions as evidence: yes/no questions (to test for the subject constituent), clefts and conjunctions (to test for the structure of the VP), negative placement, and tag questions.

Provide your five pieces of evidence in the answer sections labeled 1–5. In each case, give the following information in the spaces labeled a–d:

a. State what you are trying to show (e.g., that X is the subject constituent).
b. Provide example sentence(s) (e.g., example(s) of yes/no questions).
c. State whether the example sentence passes or fails the test.
d. State the significance of the results you found in part c.

1. a.

   b.

   c.

   d.

2. a.

   b.

   c.

   d.

3. a.

b.

c.

d.

4. a.

b.

c.

d.

5. a.

b.

c.

d.

4.9 Simple Sentences 1: German

Study the German sentences 1–25 and answer the questions that follow.

The German sentences are all in the perfective tense, which corresponds to the simple past in English: for example, *hat gemacht* "made." In English the perfective is made up of the auxiliary verb *have* and the past participle of the main verb: for example, *John has eaten.* In German the perfective is also made up of an auxiliary verb and the past participle of the main verb, but German uses two different auxiliary verbs: *haben* "to have" and *sein* "to be." The auxiliary verb *sein*, which appears in its third person singular form *ist* in this exercise, is used when the main verb refers to "motion" or a "change in state"; otherwise, the auxiliary verb is *haben*. In sentence 3, for example, the verb *fahren* "to travel," which indicates motion, appears in its third person singular perfective form with auxiliary *sein: ist gefahren*.

1. Er hat gestern eine Bemerkung gemacht.
   "He made a remark yesterday."
2. Gestern hat er eine Bemerkung gemacht.
   "Yesterday he made a remark."
3. Sie ist langsam in die Stadt gefahren.
   "She traveled into the city slowly."
4. Er hat nicht langsam gesprochen.
   "He didn't speak slowly."
5. Langsam ist sie in die Stadt gefahren.
   "Slowly she traveled into the city."
6. Gestern ist sie nicht in die Stadt gefahren.
   "Yesterday she didn't travel into the city."
7. Gefahren ist der Mann in die Stadt.
   "The man traveled into the city."
8. Den Mann hat er nicht gesehen.
   "He didn't see the man."
9. Gesehen hat eine Frau einen Mann.
   "A woman saw a man."
10. Eine Frau hat ein Mann gesehen.
    "A man saw a woman."
11. Sie hat die Bemerkung nicht gemacht.
    "She didn't make the remark."
12. Ein Mann ist nicht gegangen.
    "A man didn't go."

13. Er hat sie nicht gesehen.
   "He didn't see her."
14. Der Mann hat die Frau nicht gesehen.
   "The man didn't see the woman."
15. Der Mann ist mit der Frau gestern in die Stadt gefahren.
   "The man traveled into the city yesterday with the woman."
16. Mit der Frau ist der Mann gestern in die Stadt gefahren.
   Same as 15
17. Gestern ist der Mann mit der Frau in die Stadt gefahren.
   Same as 15
18. In die Stadt ist der Mann mit der Frau gestern gefahren.
   Same as 15
19. Sie hat keine Bemerkung gemacht.
   "She didn't make a remark."
20. Keine Bemerkung hat sie gemacht.
   Same as 19
21. Er hat die Bemerkung nicht gemacht.
   "He didn't make the remark."
22. Sie hat ihn nicht gesehen.
   "She didn't see him."
23. Die Frau hat keine Bemerkung gemacht.
   "The woman didn't make a remark."
24. Er hat keine Frau gesehen.
   "He didn't see a woman."
25. Keinen Mann hat sie gesehen.
   "She didn't see a man."

Questions

A. In German the nominative case is generally used to mark the subject of the sentence, whereas the accusative case is used to mark objects. Below, list the corresponding nominative-accusative forms that occur in this exercise. The parentheses indicate words that are not found in the data. Enter what you would predict to be the correct German forms.

	Nominative	Accusative	English gloss
1.	_____	_____	"the man"
2.	_____	_____	"a man"
3.	_____	_____	"the woman"
4.	_____	Keine Frau	"a woman"
5.	(_____)	_____	"the remark"
6.	(_____)	_____	"a remark"

7. _____ _____ "he/him"

8. _____ _____ "she/her"

B. What word in German corresponds most closely to the English word *not* (*-n't*)?

C. The overall meaning of sentences 15–18 is the same, although extra emphasis is placed on the word or phrase that is in sentence-initial position. What general property of German word order is reflected in sentences 15–18 that is also reflected in all of the other sentences in this exercise? That is, in spite of the variation in the sentences, what remains constant? Discuss particular examples to illustrate your points.

D. *Bonus.* The German system of negation is quite different from that of Modern English in a particular feature that is illustrated in the data. Note that the word *nicht* does not appear in all of the sentences that are translated into negative sentences in English. What is another form of the negative in German, and what are the conditions under which this form appears?

4.10 Simple Sentences 2: Tamil

Examine the following sentences from Tamil, a Dravidian language spoken in India, and answer the questions that follow.

1a. Na:n mi:nai va:nkukire:n.
 b. Mi:nai va:nkukire:n.
 c. Mi:nai na:n va:nkukire:n.
   "I buy the fish."

2a. Ma:lukira:n.
 b. Avan ma:lukira:n.
   "He dies."

3a. Unnai pa:rkire:n.
 b. Na:n unnai pa:rkire:n.
   "I see you."

4a. Vilukira:y.
 b. Ni: vilukira:y.
   "You fall."

5a. Karro:n a:ntiyai pa:rkira:n.
 b. A:ntiyai pa:rkira:n karro:n.
   "The teacher sees the monk."

6. Avan va:nkukira:n.
   "He buys."

7a. Avanai vaikire:n.
 b. Vaikire:n avanai na:n.
 c. Avanai vaikire:n na:n.
   "I scold him."

8a. Ni: ennai vaikira:y.
 b. Vaikira:y ennai.
   "You scold me."

9a. Manitan unnai vaikira:n.
 b. Manitan vaikira:n unnai.
   "The man scolds you."

10. Vaikira:n avanai.
   "He scolds him."

11. Avan manitanai vaikira:n.
   "He scolds the man."

12a. Karro:n ennai pa:rkira:n.
  b. Pa:rkira:n ennai karro:n.
   "The teacher sees me."

Questions

A. Isolate the Tamil morphemes, entering them in the spaces below. The parentheses indicate words that are not found in the data. Enter what you would predict to be the correct Tamil forms.

1. Verb

Tamil form	English gloss
a. _____	"buy"
b. _____	"die"
c. _____	"see"
d. _____	"fall"
e. _____	"scold"
f. _____	present tense morpheme

2. Nouns

Subject form	Object form	English gloss
a. _____	_____	"man"
b. _____	(_____)	"teacher"
c. (_____)	_____	"fish"
d. (_____)	_____	"monk"

3. Pronouns

Subject form (free)	Subject form (bound)	English gloss
a. _____	_____	"I"
b. _____	_____	"you"
c. _____	_____	"he"

	Object form (free)	English gloss
d.	_____	"me"
e.	_____	"you"
f.	_____	"him"

B. How are grammatical relations (subject, object) indicated in Tamil?

C. Discuss the role of word order (if any) in Tamil. Is it necessary to examine word order to determine the direct object in Tamil? Explain.

4.11 Simple Sentences 3: Tohono O'odham

Study the Tohono O'odham sentences 1–25 and answer the questions that follow.

The *g* before some of the words is a definite article that is close (though not identical) in meaning to the English word *the*. It never appears in sentence-initial position. The hyphen, -, indicates the sequence "prefix-stem." The asterisk, *, as usual indicates an ungrammatical sentence.

The *ñ* is an alveopalatal nasal; *č* is a voiceless alveopalatal affricate; ' is a glottal stop; *ḍ* is a voiced retroflex stop; orthographic *e* is a high back unrounded vowel (phonetically [ɨ]). A vowel with a colon after it (*iː*) is long. You may wish to consult appendix 3 for more information about the sounds in this exercise, though an exact understanding of them is not necessary to complete it successfully.

1a. S-ba:bagi 'añ ñeok.
 b. 'A:ñi 'añ ñeok s-ba:bagi.
    "I am/was speaking slowly."

2a. S-hottam 'ap čikpan.
 b. 'A:pi 'ap s-hottam čikpan.
    "You are/were working quickly."

3a. Tako 'o čičwi hegai.
 b. Čičwi 'o tako.
    "He/she was playing yesterday."

4. Čikpan 'añ 'a:ñi.
   "I am/was working."

5. 'A:pi 'ap ñeok.
   "You are/were speaking."

6a. S-ba:bagi 'o čikpan hegai.
 b. Hegai 'o s-ba:bagi čikpan.
    "He/she is/was working slowly."

7. Ñeok 'añ 'a:ñi.
   "I am/was speaking."

8. Huan 'o čeggia g Husi.
   "John is/was fighting Joe." *or*
   "Joe is/was fighting John."

9. Husi 'o g Huan čeggia.
   "John is/was fighting Joe." *or*
   "Joe is/was fighting John."

10. M-čeggia 'o g Huan.
    "John is/was fighting you."

11. Huan 'o ñ-čeggia.
    "John is/was fighting me."

12. Čeggia 'o g Husi g Huan.
    "Joe is/was fighting John." *or*
    "John is/was fighting Joe."

13. Mi:stol 'o ko:ṣ.
    "The cat is/was sleeping."

14a. 'A:ñi 'añ meḍ.
  b. Meḍ 'añ.
     "I am/was running."

15. Huan 'o čendad g Mali:ya.
    "John is/was kissing Mary." *or*
    "Mary is/was kissing John."

16. Mali:ya 'o čendad g Huan.
    "John is/was kissing Mary." *or*
    "Mary is/was kissing John."

17a. Čeoǰ 'o 'a:ñi ñ-čeggia.
  b. Ñ-čeggia 'o g čeoǰ 'a:ñi.
     "The boy is/was fighting me."

18a. Tako 'o g čeoǰ ñ-čeggia.
  b. Ñ-čeggia 'o g čeoǰ 'a:ñi tako.
     "The boy is/was fighting me yesterday."

19a. Mali:ya 'o m-čendad 'a:pi.
  b. 'A:pi 'o m-čendad g Mali:ya.
     "Mary is/was kissing you."

20a. Gogs 'o hegai huhu'id.
  b. Huhu'id 'o g gogs hegai.
     "The dog is/was chasing it/him/her."

21. M-huhu'id 'o g gogs.
    "The dog is chasing you."

22. 'A:ñi 'añ g gogs huhu'id.
    "I am/was chasing the dog."

23a. *Husi g Huan 'o čeggia.
  b. *Čeggia g Husi g Huan 'o.
  c. *'O čeggia g Husi g Huan.

24a. *Meḍ 'a:ñi 'añ.
  b. *'A:ñi meḍ 'añ.

25a. *Čikpan s-hottam 'ap.
  b. *S-hottam čikpan 'ap.

Questions

A. Write the Tohono O'odham verb morphemes corresponding to the English glosses in the spaces provided.

Tohono O'odham form	English gloss
1. _____	"fight"
2. _____	"work"
3. _____	"play"
4. _____	"sleep"
5. _____	"run"
6. _____	"kiss"
7. _____	"chase"
8. _____	"speak"

B. Tohono O'odham has auxiliary elements that mark person as well as tense/aspect. The auxiliary elements appearing in this exercise are translated into English as "*Y* is/was V-ing," where *Y* is some person or animal and V stands for the verb. List these elements in the spaces provided below.

Tohono O'odham form	English gloss
1. _____	1st person imperfect (translates as present or past progressive in English)
2. _____	2nd person imperfect
3. _____	3rd person imperfect

C. List the Tohono O'odham nouns used in this exercise.

Tohono O'odham form	English gloss
1. _____Hyan_____	"John" (Juan)
2. _____mí:stol_____	"cat"

3. _____ "boy"

4. _____ "Joe" (Jose)

5. _____ "Mary"

6. _____ "dog"

D. In sentence 13 you had to determine which word meant "cat." How did you make your decision? That is, what evidence did you bring to bear on your decision?

E. List the Tohono O'odham independent pronouns used in the example sentences.

Tohono O'odham form   English gloss

1. _____ "I/me"

2. _____hegaʼi_____ "he/him, she/her, it"

3. _____ "you"

F. Give one or two interesting properties of the Tohono O'odham independent pronouns.

G. List the Tohono O'odham adverbs corresponding to the English glosses.

Tohono O'odham form   English gloss

1. _____ "slowly"

2. _____ "quickly"

3. _____ "yesterday"

H. How are grammatical relations (subject, object) indicated in Tohono O'odham? For example, does word order play a role in determining grammatical relations? Does morphology play a role?

I. What obligatory condition on word order is true for Tohono O'odham? Be sure to take into account the ungrammatical sentences 23–25.

4.12 Simple Sentences 4: Yaqui

Yaqui is a member of the Uto-Aztecan language family and is still spoken in the Mexican state of Sonora and in southern Arizona. Examine the data below and answer the questions that follow. Italicization of the English pronoun in a translation indicates that the Yaqui pronoun is interpreted as emphatic. The asterisk preceding sentence 14 indicates that the sentence is ungrammatical.

Yaqui form	English gloss
1. Vempo uka karita veetak.	"*They* burned the house."
2. Aapo apo'ik vichak.	"*He* saw him (someone else)."
3. Aapo uka vachita itou nenkak.	"*He* sold the corn to us."
4. Inepo siika.	"*I* left."
5. Siikane.	"I left."
6. Tuukate tekipanoak.	"We worked yesterday."
7. Uka ili'uusitam aniak.	"They helped the child."
8. Siikate.	"We left."
9. Maria ab^wisek.	"Mary grabbed it."
10. Maria amb^wisek.	"Mary grabbed them."
11. Empo nee aniak.	"*You* helped *me*."
12. Peo haivu kutam chuktak.	"Pete already chopped wood."
13. Peo haivu amchuktak.	"Pete already chopped them."
14. *Peo amhaivu chuktak.	"Pete already chopped them."
15. Apo'ikne aniak.	"I helped *him*."
16. Inepo aaniak.	"*I* helped him."
17. Uka o'owtam vichak.	"They saw the man."
18. Peo uka miisita temuk.	"Pete kicked the cat."
19. U o'ow uka karita veetak.	"The man burned the house."
20. Inepo apo'ik vichak.	"*I* saw *him*."
21. U teeve o'ow maasoye'e.	"The tall man is deer-dancing."
22. Peo teeve o'owta vichak.	"Pete saw a tall man."
23. Inepo uka chukwi chuu'uta vichak.	"*I* saw the black dog."
24. Inepo enchi aniak.	"*I* helped *you*."
25. Uka karitam vichak.	"They saw the house."
26. Uka vachita'e vichak.	"You saw the corn."
27. Empo ye'ek, aapo into b^wiikak.	"*You* danced, and *he* sang."
28. Tuuka'e aniak.	"You helped yesterday."

A. In the spaces provided, write the Yaqui morphemes corresponding to the English glosses on the right. (Yaqui has a full set of pronouns for all numbers and persons, but they are not all used in this exercise.)

1. Verbs

Yaqui form	English gloss
a. _____	"burned"
b. _____	"chopped"
c. _____	"danced"
d. _____	"deer-dancing"
e. _____	"grabbed"
f. _____	"helped"
g. _____	"kicked"
h. _____	"left"
i. _____	"saw"
j. _____	"sold"
k. _____	"sang"
l. _____	"worked"

2. Full pronouns: Subject

Yaqui form	English gloss
a. _____	1st person (sg.)
b. _____	2nd person (sg.)
c. _____	3rd person (sg.)
d. _____(not in data)_____	1st person (pl.)
e. _____(not in data)_____	2nd person (pl.)
f. _____	3rd person (pl.)

3. Full pronouns: Object

	Yaqui form	English gloss
a.	_____	1st person (sg.)
b.	_____	2nd person (sg.)
c.	_____	3rd person (sg.)

4. Clitic pronouns: Subject

	Yaqui form	English gloss
a.	_____	1st person (sg.)
b.	_____	2nd person (sg.)
c.	____ (not in data) ____	3rd person (sg.)
d.	_____	1st person (pl.)
e.	____ (not in data) ____	2nd person (pl.)
d.	_____	3rd person (pl.)

5. Clitic pronouns: Object

	Yaqui form	English gloss
a.	_____	3rd person (sg.)
b.	_____	3rd person (pl.)

6. Definite articles

	Yaqui form	English gloss
a.	_____	subject
b.	_____	object

B. The *perfective* form of a Yaqui verb is translated with the English past tense. What is the most likely part of each verb that carries the meaning "perfective"? (Two verbs in sentences 1–28 do not carry this morpheme. One is inherently perfective and the other is not perfective.)

C. How are grammatical relations marked in Yaqui? Use the following terms in your answer: *subject pronouns, object pronouns, independent pronouns, case-marking suffix*. (Hint: *-po*, which looks like it might be a case-marking suffix, is not.)

D. Based on the above data, which are representative of Yaqui as a whole, discuss the word order properties of Yaqui sentences.

4.13 Simple Sentences 5: Dyirbal

The following sentences are from Dyirbal, a language spoken in North Queensland, Australia. Study the sentences carefully, and answer the questions that follow.

Do not try to account for morphological changes in the verb "hit." Also, do not try to account for the phonetic differences between the case forms of nouns and pronouns.

The unfamiliar symbols in the Dyirbal sentences represent the following sounds: ḍ is a laminopalatal/alveolar stop; ɲ is an alveopalatal nasal; ɽ is a semiretroflex, r-like sound; and ŋ is a velar nasal.

1a. balan ḍugumbil balgan
 b. balgan balan ḍugumbil
    "Someone is hitting the woman."

2a. ŋayguna balgan
 b. balgan ŋayguna
    "Someone is hitting me."

3a. bayi yaɽa yanuli
 b. yanuli bayi yaɽa
    "The man has to go out."

4a. balan ḍugumbil baŋgul yaɽaŋgu balgan
 b. balgan balan ḍugumbil baŋgul yaɽaŋgu
 c. baŋgul yaɽaŋgu balgan balan ḍugumbil
 d. balan ḍugumbil balgan baŋgul yaɽaŋgu
 e. balgan baŋgul yaɽaŋgu balan ḍugumbil
 f. baŋgul yaɽaŋgu balan ḍugumbil balgan
    "The man is hitting the woman."

5. bayi yaɽa baŋgun ḍugumbiru balgan
   "The woman is hitting the man."

6a. ŋaḍa balgalŋaɲu
 b. balgalŋaɲu ŋaḍa
    "I am hitting someone."

7a. balan ḍugumbil badiɲu
 b. badiɲu balan ḍugumbil
    "The woman falls down."

8a. ŋaḍa ŋinuna balgan
 b. ŋinuna ŋaḍa balgan
 c. balgan ŋaḍa ŋinuna
 d. balgan ŋinuna ŋaḍa
 e. ŋaḍa balgan ŋinuna
 f. ŋinuna balgan ŋaḍa
    "I'm hitting you."

9. bayi yaṛa balgalŋuɲu
   "The man is hitting someone."

10. ŋinda ŋayguna balgan
    "You're hitting me."

11. ŋaḍa bayi yaṛa balgan
    "I'm hitting the man."

12. bayi yaṛa yanu
    "The man is going."

13. bayi bargan baŋgul yaṛaŋgu ḍurgaɲu
    "The man is spearing the wallaby."

14. ŋayguna baŋgul yaṛaŋgu balgan
    "The man is hitting me."

15. bayi yaṛa baniɲu
    "The man is coming."

16. balan ḍugumbil yanu
    "The woman is going."

17. balan ḍugumbil baniɲu
    "The woman is coming."

18. ŋinda baniɲu
    "You are coming."

19. ŋaḍa baniɲu
    "I am coming."

Questions

A. Begin your analysis by filling in the spaces below with the appropriate Dyirbal forms.

1. Subject of transitive sentence

   Dyirbal form   English gloss

   a. _____ "the man"

   b. _____ "the woman"

2. Object of transitive sentence

    Dyirbal form   English gloss

 a. _____ "the man"

 b. _____ "the woman"

 c. _____ "the wallaby"

3. Subject of intransitive sentence

    Dyirbal form   English gloss

 a. _____ "the man"

 b. _____ "the woman"

B. English and almost all European languages are classified as "nominative/accusative." In a nominative/accusative language the subject of a transitive sentence is marked in the same way as the subject of an intransitive sentence, but the object of a transitive sentence is marked differently. In English this difference shows up in the pronominal system. For example, *she* (the nominative form of the third person singular feminine pronoun) is used as the subject of both transitive and intransitive sentences; *her* (the object or accusative form of the third person singular feminine pronoun) is used in object position. Thus, *She hit the ball*, *She ran*, but *The fans watched her*.

In contrast, some of the world's languages—among them Dyirbal—are classified as "ergative/absolutive" languages. What property of the Dyirbal example sentences distinguishes Dyirbal from nominative/accusative languages? In other words, what property defines an ergative/absolutive language as opposed to a nominative/accusative language? Limit yourself to the words displayed in question A.

C. Although Dyirbal is classified as an ergative/absolute language, it is more precisely defined as a "split ergative" language. To learn what a split ergative language is, begin by filling in the spaces below.

    1. Subject of transitive sentence

        Dyirbal form   English gloss

        a. _____   "I"

        b. _____   "you"

    2. Object of transitive sentence

        Dyirbal form   English gloss

        a. _____   "me"

        b. _____   "you"

    3. Subject of intransitive sentence

        Dyirbal form   English gloss

        a. _____   "I"

        b. _____   "you"

D. Noting the contrast between the first and second person pronouns in questions C-1 through C-3 and the nouns in questions A-1 through A-3, state what you think the properties of a split ergative language are. For example, are subject and object marked the same way on nouns as they are on pronouns?

4.14 Simple Sentences 6: Japanese

Examine the Japanese sentences 1–7 and answer the questions that follow.

Assume that the particles -ga, -o, and -ni indicate whether the noun phrase to which they are attached is functioning as subject, object, or indirect object, respectively.

1a. Sono kodomo-ga tokei-o mita.
 b. Tokei-o sono kodomo-ga mita.
   "That child saw the watch."

2. Sono tokei-ga ookii desu.
   "That watch is big."

3a. Kare-no hahaoya-o otoko-ga aisita.
 b. Otoko-ga kare-no hahaoya-o aisita.
   "The man loved his mother."

4. Watasi-no hahaoya-ga sinda.
   "My mother died."

5a. Watasi-no kodomo-ni sensei-ga sono hon-o ageta.
 b. Sensei-ga watasi-no kodomo-ni sono hon-o ageta.
 c. Sono hon-o sensei-ga watasi-no kodomo-ni ageta.
 d. Sono hon-o watasi-no kodomo-ni sensei-ga ageta.
   "The teacher gave that book to my child."

6a. Kare-ga sono hon-o katta.
 b. Sono hon-o kare-ga katta.
   "He bought that book."

7a. Watasi-ga sono enpitu-o katta.
 b. Sono enpitu-o watasi-ga katta.
   "I bought that pencil."

Questions

A. Provide the Japanese equivalents to the English words below.

Japanese form   English gloss

1. _____ "child"

2. _____ "watch"

3. _____ "man"

4. _____ "mother"

5. _____ "book"

6. _____ "I"

7. _____ "pencil"

8. _____ "saw"

9. _____ "is"

10. _____ "loved"

11. _____ "that"

12. _____ "big"

13. _____ "he"

14. _____ "died"

B. How is the possessive formed in Japanese? (Examine sentences 3, 4, and 5.)

C. How would you translate *that man's child* into Japanese?

D. What constraints do there appear to be on word order in Japanese? (Be sure to examine all the variations on word order in sentences 1–7 before answering this question. You will find some elements whose order never varies.)

E. What is the Japanese sentence for *That mother's child gave the watch to that child*?

4.15 Complex Sentences 1: Japanese

In the following examples from Japanese, the a-sentences are simple sentences and each b-sentence contains a relative clause based on the corresponding a-sentence. Examine the sentences and answer questions A–E.

When -*wa* appears, it marks the subject of the verb of the main clause of the sentence; otherwise, the subject is marked with -*ga*. Furthermore, assume that -*o* indicates direct object.

1a. Kinoo John-ga otoko-o nagutta.
   "Yesterday, John hit a man."
 b. Watasi-wa kinoo John-ga nagutta otoko-o mita.
   "I saw the man whom John hit yesterday."

2a. Kinoo John-ga otoko-o nagutta.
   "Yesterday, John hit a man."
 b. Kinoo John-ga nagutta otoko-ga paatii-ni kita.
   "The man whom John hit yesterday came to the party."

3a. Kinoo otoko-ga John-o nagutta.
   "Yesterday, a man hit John."
 b. Watasi-wa kinoo John-o nagutta otoko-o mita.
   "I saw the man who hit John yesterday."

4a. Watasi-wa Hanako-kara hon-o karita.
   "I borrowed a book from Hanako."
 b. Otooto-wa watasi-ga Hanako-kara karita hon-o nakusita.
   "My brother lost the book which I borrowed from Hanako."

5a. Watasi-wa Hanako-kara hon-o karita.
   "I borrowed a book from Hanako."
 b. Watasi-ga Hanako-kara karita hon-wa totemo omosiroi.
   "The book which I borrowed from Hanako is very interesting."

Questions

A. Provide the Japanese equivalents for the English words and phrases below.

Japanese form   English gloss

1. _____ "hit"

2. _____ "I"

3. _____ "is interesting"

4. _____ "came"

5. _____ "book"

6. _____ "man"

7. _____ "very"

8. _____ "to"

9. _____ "lost"

10. _____ "saw"

11. _____ "party"

12. _____ "yesterday"

13. _____ "borrowed"

14. _____ "(my) brother"

15. _____ "from"

B. In English a relative clause may be introduced by a relative pronoun such as *who* or *which* (*the book which you borrowed*). Does Japanese have such a word that indicates the presence of a relative clause?

C. In the noun phrase *the child who cried a lot*, *the child* is called the "head" of the relative clause. In English the "head" occurs to the left of the relative clause. Where does the "head" of the relative clause occur in a Japanese noun phrase?

D. For each of the b-sentences, draw brackets around the noun phrase that contains the relative clause. Be sure to put the relative clause within the brackets for the noun phrase in the following manner:

1b. Watasi -wa [NP kinoo John -ga nagutta otoko NP] -o mita.

   "I saw the man whom John hit yesterday."

2b. Kinoo John -ga nagutta otoko -ga paatii -ni kita.

   "The man whom John hit yesterday came to the party."

3b. Watasi -wa kinoo John -o nagutta otoko -o mita.

   "I saw the man who hit John yesterday."

4b. Otooto -wa watasi -ga Hanako -kara karita hon -o nakusita.

   "My brother lost the book which I borrowed from Hanako."

5b. Watasi -ga Hanako -kara karita hon -wa totemo omosiroi.

   "The book which I borrowed from Hanako is very interesting."

E. Translate the noun phrase *the book which (my) brother lost* into Japanese.

4.16 Complex Sentences 2: Modern Irish

In Modern Irish the complementizer (subordinating conjunction) appearing in relative clauses has two forms, distinguished not in the actual form the complementizer takes (it is always simply *a*, in the cases we will consider) but in the consonant mutations induced in the immediately following verb-initial consonant. These mutations are *lenition* and *eclipsis*. Lenition (or aspiration) is indicated by *h* following the verb-initial consonant: $c \rightarrow ch$, $f \rightarrow fh$, and so on. Eclipsis is symbolized by writing a nasal or voiced consonant before the verb-initial consonant or, in the case of some consonants, by leaving it unaffected: $c \rightarrow gc$, $f \rightarrow bhf$, $m \rightarrow m$, $g \rightarrow ng$, and so on.

Examples 1–20 contain Irish sentences that are paired with corresponding relative clauses derived from closely analogous sentences. Study the sentences carefully, paying particular attention to the distribution of the two forms of the complementizer, and answer the questions that follow.

1a. Díolann an fear capaill.
   (sells the man horses)
   "The man sells horses."
  b. an fear a dhíolann capaill
   (the man COMP sells horses)
   "the man who sells horses"

2a. Molann Seán an tír.
   (praises John the country)
   "John praises the country."
  b. an tír a mholann Seán
   "the country that John praises"

3a. Cónaíonn Seán le fir.
   (lives John with men)
   "John lives with men."
  b. na fir a gcónaíonn Seán leo
   (the men COMP lives John with-them)
   "the men John lives with"
  c. *na fir a chónaíonn Seán le

4a. Díolann cara an fhir capaill.
   (sells friend of-the man horses)
   "The man's friend sells horses."

b. an fear a ndíolann a chara capaill
   (the man COMP sells his friend horses)
   "the man whose friend sells horses"

c. *an fear a dhíolann cara capaill

5a. Díolann Seán agus an fear capaill.
    (sells John and the man horses)
    "John and the man sell horses."

b. an fear a ndíolann Seán agus é féin capaill.
   "the man that John and him himself sell horses"

c. *an fear a dhíolann Seán agus capaill

6a. Feicim an fear a mholann an tír.
    (I-see the man COMP praises the country)
    "I see the man who praises the country."

b. an tír a bhfeicim an fear a mholann í
   (the land COMP I-see the man COMP praises it)
   "the country that I see the man who praises it"

c. *an tír a fheicim an fear a mholann

7a. Feicim an tír a mholann an fear.
    "I see the country that the man praises."

b. an fear a bhfeicim an tír a mholann sé
   "the man that I see the country that he praises"

c. *an fear a fheicim an tír a mholann

8a. Feicim na fir a gcónaíonn an buachaill seo leo.
    (I-see the men COMP lives the boy this with-them)
    "I see the men that this boy lives with."

b. an buachaill a bhfeicim na fir a gcónaíonn sé leo
   "the boy that I see the men that he lives with"

c. *an buachaill a fheicim na fir a gcónaíonn leo

9a. Ceapann Seán go ndíolann an fear seo capaill.
    (thinks John COMP sells the man these horses)
    "John thinks that this man sells horses."

b. an fear a cheapann Seán a dhíolann capaill
   "the man that John thinks sells horses"

c. an fear a gceapann Seán go ndíolann sé capaill
   "the man that John thinks sells horses"

10a. Ceapann Seán go molann Pádraig an tír seo.
     (thinks John COMP praises Patrick the country this)
     "John thinks that Patrick praises this country."

b. an tír a cheapann Seán a mholann Pádraig
   "the country that John thinks Patrick praises"

c. an tír a gceapann Seán go molann Pádraig í
   (the country COMP thinks John COMP praises Patrick it)
   "the country that John thinks Patrick praises"

146

11a. Ceapann Seán go gcónaíonn Pádraig le fir.
"John thinks that Patrick lives with men."

b. na fir a gceapann Seán go gcónaíonn Pádraig leo
(the men COMP thinks John COMP lives Patrick with-them)
"the men that John thinks Patrick lives with"

c. *na fir a cheapann Seán a chónaíonn Pádraig le

12. Feiceann Seán Máire i mBoston gach lá.
"John sees Mary in Boston every day."

13. Feiceann Seán i mBoston gach lá í.
(sees John in Boston every day her)
"John sees her in Boston every day."

14. Feiceann sé Máire i mBoston gach lá.
(sees he Mary in Boston every day)
"He sees Mary in Boston every day."

15. Feiceann sé i mBoston gach lá í.
"He sees her in Boston every day."

16. an bhean a fheiceann Seán i mBoston gach lá.
"the woman that John sees in Boston every day"

17. an bhean a bhfeiceann Seán i mBoston gach lá í
"the woman that John sees in Boston every day"

18. *an fear a ndíolann sé capaill
(the man COMP sells he horses)

19. na capaill a dhíolann an fear
"the horses that the man sells"

20. na capaill a ndíolann an fear iad
(the horses COMP sells the man them)
"the horses that the man sells"

Questions

A. Identify the various verb forms in Irish by filling in the blanks below.

Irish form   English gloss

1. _____   "sells"

   _____

   _____

2. _____ "praises"

_____

3. _____ "lives"

_____

4. _____ "sees"

_____

_____ 1st person

_____ 3rd person

5. _____ "thinks"

_____

_____

B. Identify the following Irish phrases.

   Irish form   English gloss

1. _____ "the man"

2. _____ "the men"

3. _____ "with them"

4. _____ "the country"

5. _____ "this man"

6. _____ "with men"

7. _____ "horses"

8. _____ "this country"

C. What syntactic properties determine when the verb-initial consonant undergoes lenition (aspiration)?

D. What syntactic properties determine when the verb-initial consonant is affected by eclipsis?

E. Why are sentences 3c and 5c ungrammatical?

F. Why are sentences 6c and 7c ungrammatical?

G. Why is sentence 8c ungrammatical?

H. Why is sentence 18 ungrammatical?

I. Give an analysis of Irish relative clauses that will (1) account for the distribution of the two forms of the complementizer and (2) explain the grammaticality judgments indicated in examples 1–20.

Name _____

Section _____

4.17 Morphosyntax 1: Telugu

Each of the following words in Telugu (a Dravidian language spoken in India) is translated into English by an entire sentence. Each word is complex, that is, composed of several morphemes. Analyze the words by identifying the morphemes occurring in each word, and answer questions A–C.

The phonetic values of the symbols used can be determined from the chart in appendix 3. An exact understanding of the value of the phonetic symbols is not necessary to carry out the analysis required for this exercise. For example, the *d* with a dot under it (*ḍ*) can be understood simply as a "different kind of *d*" that appears in Telugu but not in English.

The verbal morphology of Telugu is very complex, a fact that is not reflected in this exercise.

	Telugu form	English gloss
1.	ceppɛɛnu	"I told"
2.	ceppincunu	"I cause (someone) to tell"
3.	cuustaam	"We will see"
4.	ceppɛɛm	"We told"
5.	ceppanu	"I will not tell"
6.	navvincum	"We cause (someone) to laugh"
7.	cuustunnaaḍu	"He is seeing"
8.	ceppɛɛyi	"They told"
9.	koḍataanu	"I will beat"
10.	paaḍataanu	"I will sing"
11.	ceppɛɛru	"You (pl.) told"
12.	ceppavu	"You (sg.) will not tell"
13.	ceppɛɛvu	"You (sg.) told"
14.	ceppam	"We will not tell"
15.	ceppɛɛḍu	"He told"
16.	cuusɛɛḍu	"He saw"
17.	cepparu	"You (pl.) will not tell"
18.	koḍatunnaayi	"They are beating"
19.	ceestunnaanu	"I am doing"
20.	aḍugutaam	"We will ask"
21.	ceesɛɛnu	"I did"
22.	aḍugutaaḍu	"He will ask"

Questions

A. In the spaces below, list the Telugu morphemes that correspond to the English words on the right.

1. Verbs

Telugu morpheme	English gloss
a. _____	"tell"
b. _____	"sing"
c. _____	"see"
d. _____	"laugh"
e. _____	"ask"
f. _____	"beat"
g. _____	"do"

2. Person marking of subjects

Telugu morpheme	English gloss
a. _____	"I"
b. _____	"you (sg.)"
c. _____	"he"
d. _____	"we"
e. _____	"you (pl.)"
f. _____	"they"

3. Others

Telugu morpheme	English gloss
a. _____	past tense
b. _____	present tense (-*ing* form in English gloss)
c. _____	future tense
d. _____	negative future tense
e. _____	causative

B. List the order in which the morphemes occur in the Telugu words. (For example, in *ceppεεnu*, which morpheme comes first? The verb? The subject? Tense?) Use terms such as *causative, tense, subject, verb*.

C. Translate the following English sentences into Telugu.

1. You (pl.) are singing. _____

2. They will not laugh. _____

3. You (sg.) will cause (someone) to ask. _____

4.18 Morphosyntax 2: Swahili

As was true of the Telugu words in exercise 4.17, each of the following words in Swahili (a language of the Niger-Congo family spoken in Africa) is translated into English by an entire sentence. Each word is complex, that is, composed of several morphemes. Analyze the forms by identifying the morphemes occurring in each word, and answer the questions that follow.

	Swahili form	English gloss
1.	aliwaandika	"He/she wrote you (pl.)"
2.	ninakujua	"I know you (sg.)"
3.	anasoma	"He/she reads"
4.	ulituuliza	"You (sg.) asked us"
5.	tulikuona	"We saw you (sg.)"
6.	anamjua	"He/she knows him/her"
7.	mtasoma	"You (pl.) will read"
8.	walimpiga	"They hit him/her" (past)
9.	umeandika	"You (sg.) have just written"
10.	mlimpiga	"You (pl.) hit him/her" (past)
11.	anakujua	"He/she knows you (sg.)"
12.	mtaniona	"You (pl.) will see me"
13.	nimembusu	"I have just kissed him/her"
14.	walisoma	"They read" (past)
15.	nitawabusu	"I will kiss you (pl.)"
16.	tumewaandika	"We have just written you (pl.)"
17.	utanibusu	"You (sg.) will kiss me"
18.	utatupiga	"You (sg.) will hit us"
19.	wamewauliza	"They have just asked them"
20.	tumewauliza	"We have just asked them"

A. In the spaces below, list the Swahili morphemes that correspond to the English words on the right.

1. Subjects

Swahili morpheme	English gloss
a. _____	"I"
b. _____	"you (sg.)"
c. _____	"he/she"
d. _____	"we"
e. _____	"you (pl.)"
f. _____	"they"

2. Objects

Swahili morpheme	English gloss
a. _____	"me"
b. _____	"you (sg.)"
c. _____	"him/her"
d. _____	"us"
e. _____	"you (pl.)"
f. _____	"them"

3. "Tenses"

Swahili morpheme	English gloss
a. _____	present
b. _____	future
c. _____	past
d. _____	recent perfective ("have just *X*'d")

4. Verbs

	Swahili morpheme	English gloss
a.	_____	"write"
b.	_____	"ask"
c.	_____	"read"
d.	_____	"see"
e.	_____	"know"
f.	_____	"hit"
g.	_____	"kiss"

B. List the order in which morphemes occur in the Swahili words given in examples 1–20. Use terms such as *verb*, *subject*, and *object*.

C. *Bonus*. The morphemes for second person plural subjects and third person singular objects involve a certain phonological complication: as examples 21–25 show, each morpheme appears in two different forms, and the shape that occurs in a particular word can be predicted from the phonological environment (the surrounding sounds) in which the morpheme appears.

The forms in 24 and 25 contain another present tense marker, -*a*-, which indicates that the action of the verb either is an established state or is generally the case. The English present tense is very close in meaning to the Swahili tense marked with -*a*-.

21.	nilimwandika	"I wrote him/her"
22.	tulimwona	"We saw him/her"
23.	unamwuliza	"You (sg.) ask him/her"
24.	mwamwandika	"You (pl.) write him/her"
25.	mwasoma	"You (pl.) read"

Considering examples 21–25 and referring back to examples 1–20, describe the environment that conditions the appearance of each of the two forms in the most general statement you can devise.

4.19 Morphosyntax 3: Classical Nahuatl (Aztec)

Isolate the morphemes for the following forms of Classical Nahuatl (a Uto-Aztecan language spoken in Mexico) and answer questions A–D.

This exercise introduces a new feature. Sometimes in a language, as in Nahuatl, the lack of an overt morpheme has meaning. Some of the examples in 1–21, then, will have an element of meaning for which no phonetically realized morpheme is present. Represent these phonetically empty morphemes in the appropriate spaces below with ∅ (the symbol used by linguists to indicate such morphemes).

This exercise uses an alphabet somewhat different from the one Nahuatl speakers use to write the modern language. The current Nahuatl alphabet is based on the conventions used to write Spanish. In this exercise (as in the current Nahuatl alphabet) the letters *ch* correspond to the sound represented by *ch* in English, as in the word *chip* (see *Linguistics*, p. 77). A colon following a vowel indicates that the vowel is long.

	Nahuatl form	English gloss
1.	nicho:ka	"I cry"
2.	nicho:kani	"I am crying"
3.	ankochinih	"You (pl.) are sleeping"
4.	tikochih	"We sleep"
5.	kochiya	"He was sleeping"
6.	kwi:kas	"He will sing"
7.	ankochiyah	"You (pl.) were sleeping"
8.	nicho:kas	"I will cry"
9.	cho:kayah	"They were crying"
10.	tikochi	"You (sg.) sleep"
11.	ancho:kah	"You (pl.) cry"
12.	tikochis	"You (sg.) will sleep"
13.	ticho:kayah	"We were crying"
14.	cho:ka	"He cries"
15.	kochini	"He is sleeping"
16.	ancho:kayah	"You (pl.) were crying"
17.	ticho:kanih	"We are crying"
18.	kwi:kah	"They sing"
19.	tikwi:kani	"You (sg.) are singing"
20.	nikwi:kaya	"I was singing"
21.	cho:kanih	"They are crying"

A. In the spaces below, list the Classical Nahuatl morphemes that correspond to the English words on the right.

1. Verbs

Nahuatl morpheme	English gloss
a. _____	"sleep"
b. _____	"sing"
c. _____	"cry"

2. Person marking (for subject)

Nahuatl morpheme	English gloss
a. _____	"I"
b. _____	"you (sg.)"
c. _____	"he"
d. _____ _____	"we"
e. _____ _____	"you (pl.)"
f. _____ _____	"they"

3. Tense marking

Nahuatl morpheme	English gloss
a. _____	present
b. _____	customary present (corresponds in English to the present progressive—that is, -*ing* forms)
c. _____	imperfect (translated in English as a past progressive—that is, "was V-ing," where V stands for any verb)
d. _____	future

B. Give the order of the morphemes in Nahuatl, using the category labels found in question A (*verb*, *subject*, *tense*, etc.).

C. Translate the following Nahuatl forms into English.

1. tikwi:ka   _____

2. cho:kani   _____

3. nikochiya   _____

D. Translate the following English sentences into Nahuatl.

1. You (sg.) are sleeping.   _____

2. They will sing.   _____

3. We cry.   _____

4.20 Morphosyntax 4: Merkin

Analyze the following sentences and answer the questions that follow. In this language, the words on the left correspond to the English sentences on the right. Compare the properties of Merkin with those of Telugu and Swahili (exercises 4.17 and 4.18). For symbols that may be unfamiliar to you, refer to appendix 3 or to chapter 3 in *Linguistics*.

	Merkin form	English gloss
1.	ɑlhɪdəm	"I will hit him/them"
2.	ʃɪlsi	"She will see"
3.	wɪlteɪkɪt	"We will take it"
4.	hidhɪdəm	"He would hit him/them"
5.	jusiəm	"You see him/them"
6.	ɑlsiɚ	"I will see her"
7.	ɑlsiɨt	"I will see it"
8.	ʃidsiəm	"She would see him/them"
9.	ðɛlnoʊəm	"They will know him/them"
10.	wɪlnoʊɨt	"We will know it"
11.	ɪdɨdteɪkɪt	"It would take it"
12.	ðeɪdlʌvɚ	"They would love her"
13.	hidlʌvəm	"He would love him/them"
14.	hɪlnoʊɚ	"He will know her"
15.	aɪdlʌvɨt	"I would love it"
16.	ɪdɨdteɪkɚ	"It would take her"
17.	jʊlhɪdəm	"You will hit him/them"
18.	hidnoʊəm	"He would know him/them"
19.	widteɪkɪt	"We would take it"
20.	ðɛlnoʊəm	"They will know him/them"
21.	judhɪdɚ	"You would hit her"
22.	ɪdəlsiɚ	"It will see her"

Questions

A. In the spaces below, list the Merkin morphemes that correspond to the English translations.

1. Verbs

   Merkin morpheme   English gloss

   a. _____ "hit"

   b. _____ "love"

   c. _____ "know"

   d. _____ "take"

   e. _____ "see"

2. Subject marking

   Merkin morpheme   English gloss

   a. _____ 1st person singular

   _____

   b. _____ 2nd person singular

   _____

   c. _____ 3rd person singular masculine

   _____

   d. _____ 3rd person singular feminine

   _____

   e. _____ 3rd person singular inanimate

   f. _____ 1st person plural

   _____

   g. _____ 3rd person plural

   _____

164

3. Object marking

Merkin morpheme	English gloss
a. _____	3rd person singular masculine
b. _____	3rd person singular feminine
c. _____	3rd person singular inanimate
d. _____	3rd person plural

4. Modality marking

Merkin morpheme	English gloss
a. _____	future
_____	
b. _____	conditional
_____	

B. What is the word order in a Merkin sentence? Use terms such as *subject*, *object*, *verb*.

C. The subject-marking morphemes occur in both a long and a short form. What is the conditioning environment for each form?

D. The modality morphemes occur in both a long and a short form. What is the conditioning environment for each form?

4.21 Special Topic 1: C-Command

Consider the following tree and answer questions A–F:

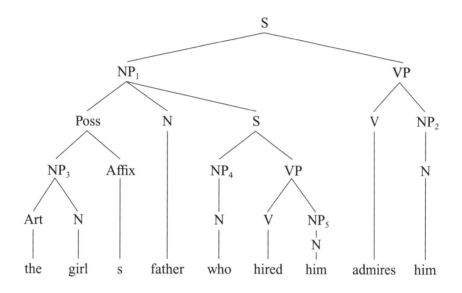

Assume the following definition of c(onstituent)-command (see also *Linguistics*, p. 214):

Node A c-commands node B if and only if the first branching node that dominates A also dominates B (condition: A does not dominate B and vice versa).

Questions

A. Does NP₁ c-command NP₂? Why or why not?

B. Does NP₂ c-command NP₁? Why or why not?

C. Does NP$_1$ c-command NP$_3$? Why or why not?

D. Does NP$_5$ c-command NP$_2$? Why or why not?

E. Assume that *him* and *John* can be used to refer to the same individual in the sentence *The girl's father who hired him admires John.* Does *John* have to c-command the pronoun *him* in order to be coreferential with it? Explain.

F. Provide another example sentence where a pronoun occurs before a noun phrase, such as *John*, and is coreferential with it.

4.22 Special Topic 2: Reflexive (English)

The following quotation is taken from an English grammar book:

Limitations on Active-Passive Conversions:
You should be aware that not all actives with direct objects can be converted into passives. Actives in which the direct object is a reflexive do not convert successfully. "He hated himself" converts into the unacceptable *"Himself was hated by him." (Cook and Suter 1980, 75)

If the unacceptability of *Himself was hated by him is accounted for by saying that an active cannot be converted into a passive when the direct object is a reflexive, then sentences like those given below would presumably involve a different kind of oddity since they are *not* active-passive pairs.

1a. John loves himself.
 b. Himself loves John. (odd)

2a. Mary looked at herself in the mirror.
 b. Herself looked at Mary in the mirror. (odd)

3a. The bosses paid themselves adequately.
 b. Themselves paid the bosses adequately. (odd)

4a. Mary forced John to wash himself.
 b. Mary forced himself to wash John. (odd with *John = himself*)

5a. Mary expected John to wash himself.
 b. Mary expected himself to wash John. (odd with *himself = John*)

However, the odd b-sentences and the passive sentence *Himself was hated by him* do in fact have something in common. Study these sentences and answer questions A–C.

Questions

A. What do the b-sentences of 1–5 and the passive sentence *Himself was hated by him* have in common?

B. Check your answer to question A against the data below. What revisions are necessary in order to account for the new data? (Review *Linguistics*, pp. 206–209 and 213–215.)

6a. The man believes that himself will win.   (odd)
 b. The man believes that he will win.

7a. The man loves the woman who admires himself.   (odd)
 b. The man loves the woman who admires him.

8a. That the boy likes herself pleased the girl.   (odd)
 b. That the boy likes her pleased the girl.

9a. The boy knows that himself told the truth.   (odd)
 b. The boy knows that he told the truth.

10a. The girl who saw himself knows the man.   (odd)
 b. The girl who saw him knows the man.

C. An account of the unacceptability of *Himself was hated by him* that is based on the assumption that an active cannot be converted into a passive when the direct object is a reflexive misses something important. Provide a more general account for the oddity of the b-sentences in 1–5 and the a-sentences in 6–10 that subsumes the passive example. (Hint: Review exercise 4.21.)

4.23 Special Topic 3: Reflexive (Russian)

Study the Russian sentences in lists I and II and answer the questions that follow.
  For the purposes of the exercise, ignore the prefix on the verb in sentence 6.
  The prepositions used in this exercise are *ot* "from," *k* "for," *pod* "under," and *v* "in."

List I	List II
1. Ya ukryl detei ot solntsa. "I hid the children from the sun."	Ya ukrylsya ot solntsa. "I hid myself from the sun."
2. On gotovil detei k ekzamenu. "He prepared the children for the exam."	On gotovilsya k ekzamenu. "He prepared himself for the exam."
3. On videl detei pod stolom. "He saw the children under the table."	On videlsya v zerkalo. "He saw himself in the mirror."
4. On kupal detei. "He bathed the children."	On kupalsya. "He bathed himself."
5. On odeval detei. "He dressed the children."	On odevalsya. "He dressed himself."
6. On rezal xleb. "He cut the bread."	On porezalsya. "He cut himself."
7. On prichesal detei. "He combed the children."	On prichesalsya. "He combed himself (his hair)."
8. On xotel ubit' zayatsa. "He wanted to kill a rabbit."	On xotel ubitsya. "He wanted to kill himself."

Questions

A. Write the Russian words corresponding to the English glosses.

Russian form	English gloss
1. _____	"table"
2. _____	"I"
3. _____	"he"

4. _____ "sun"

5. _____ "children"

6. _____ "exam"

7. _____ "bread"

8. _____ "mirror"

9. _____ "rabbit"

B. The verbs (except for *xotel*) appear in two forms. For each verb listed below, provide the two forms.

Shorter form   Longer form

1. _____   _____ "hid"

2. _____   _____ "prepared"

3. _____   _____ "saw"

4. _____   _____ "bathed"

5. _____   _____ "dressed"

6. _____   _____ "cut"

7. _____   _____ "combed"

8. _____   _____ "kill"

C. When does the longer form of the verb occur? That is, state the conditioning environment for the longer form of the verb.

D. When does the shorter form of the verb occur? Under what conditions?

4.24 Special Topic 4: Reflexive (Japanese)

Study the sentences in lists I and II and answer the questions that follow.

Assume that the particles *-wa*, *-o*, and *-ni* mark subject, object, and indirect object, respectively. (Note: *Taroo* is a man's name and *Mieko* is a woman's name.)

List I	List II
1a. Taroo-wa Mieko-o sinraisiteiru.	1a. Taroo-wa zibun-o sinraisiteiru.
b. Mieko-o Taroo-wa sinraisiteiru.	b. Zibun-o Taroo-wa sinraisiteiru.
"Taro trusts Mieko."	"Taro trusts himself."
2a. Taroo-wa Mieko-o hihansita.	2a. Taroo-wa zibun-o hihansita.
b. Mieko-o Taroo-wa hihansita.	b. Zibun-o Taroo-wa hihansita.
"Taro criticized Mieko."	"Taro criticized himself."
3a. Taroo-wa Mieko-o sensei-ni urikonda.	3a. Taroo-wa zibun-o sensei-ni urikonda.
b. Mieko-o Taroo-wa sensei-ni urikonda.	b. Zibun-o Taroo-wa sensei-ni urikonda.
"Taro presented Mieko to the teacher."	"Taro presented himself to the teacher."
4a. Mieko-wa Taroo-o aisiteiru.	4a. Mieko-wa zibun-o aisiteiru.
b. Taroo-o Mieko-wa aisiteiru.	b. Zibun-o Mieko-wa aisiteiru.
"Mieko loves Taro."	"Mieko loves herself."
5a. Mieko-wa Taroo-o keibetsusiteiru.	5a. Mieko-wa zibun-o keibetsusiteiru.
b. Taroo-o Mieko-wa keibetsusiteiru.	b. Zibun-o Mieko-wa keibetsusiteiru.
"Mieko despises Taro."	"Mieko despises herself."
6a. Taroo-wa Mieko-o tataita.	6a. Taroo-wa zibun-o tataita.
b. Mieko-o Taroo-wa tataita.	b. Zibun-o Taroo-wa tataita.
"Taro hit Mieko."	"Taro hit himself."

A. Provide the Japanese equivalents to the English words below by filling in the blanks.

Japanese form   English gloss

1. _____ "presented"

2. _____ "criticized"

3. _____ "trusts"

4. _____ "loves"

5. _____ "despises"

6. _____ "hit"

7. _____ "teacher"

B. The word *zibun* translates into English as the reflexive *himself/herself*. Given data in 1–6, what differences do you find between the English reflexive and *zibun*? (Hint: Compare where the "reflexive" words occur, their morphologic form, and so forth.) In answering this question, you may find it useful to consult the previous exercises on reflexives.

4.25 Special Topic 5: Reflexive (Japanese)

In this exercise you will be exploring the use of the Japanese reflexive *zibun* in embedded (subordinate) clauses. Examine sentences 1–3 and answer the questions that follow.

In these examples the particle *-wa* marks the subject of the verb of the main clause of the sentence, and *-ga* marks the subject of the embedded clause.

1a. Taroo-wa Hanako-ga zibun-o aisiteiru to omotteimasu.
    "Taro thinks that Hanako loves herself." *or*
    "Taro thinks that Hanako loves him (Taro)."
  b. Taroo-wa zibun-ga Hanako-o aisiteiru to omotteimasu.
    "Taro thinks that he (Taro) loves Hanako."

2a. Taroo-wa Hanako-ga zibun-o mita to itta.
    "Taro said that Hanako saw herself." *or*
    "Taro said that Hanako saw him (Taro)."
  b. Taroo-wa zibun-ga Hanako-o mita to itta.
    "Taro said that he (Taro) saw Hanako."

3a. Taroo-wa Hanako-ga zibun-o hihansita to sinziteiru.
    "Taro believes that Hanako criticized herself." *or*
    "Taro believes that Hanako criticized him (Taro)."
  b. Taroo-wa zibun-ga Hanako-o hihansita to sinziteiru.
    "Taro believes that he (Taro) criticized Hanako."

Questions

A. Provide the Japanese equivalents to the English words below by filling in the blanks.

Japanese form	English gloss
1. _____	"thinks"
2. _____	"believes"
3. _____	"said"
4. _____	"that"

B. Sentences 1a, 2a, and 3a all have two interpretations with respect to *zibun*. What is the difference between these two interpretations? Pay close attention to the English translations that have been provided.

C. None of the b-sentences are ambiguous in the way the a-sentences are. What is the syntactic difference between the two sets of sentences that accounts for the fact that the b-sentences have only one interpretation, whereas the a-sentences have two?

D. Review exercise 4.22 on the English reflexive, especially question B. Compare and contrast Japanese *zibun* with English *himself/herself*. Consider the restrictions on the relative positions of the "antecedent" (*Taroo* in example 6 of exercise 4.24) and the "anaphor" (*zibun* and *himself/herself*) as well as any special restrictions one language might have on the "antecedent" with regard to grammatical relations.

5 Semantics

5.1 Compositional and Noncompositional Meanings

The cartoon accompanying each of the following expressions depicts its compositional meaning—that is, the meaning determined by putting together the meanings of its parts. However, each expression also has a noncompositional (idiomatic) meaning. Consider the expressions and the compositional meanings depicted by the cartoons; you will be asked to supply their noncompositional meanings.

1. He's sitting on the fence.

2. They put the cart before the horse.

3. He's barking up the wrong tree.

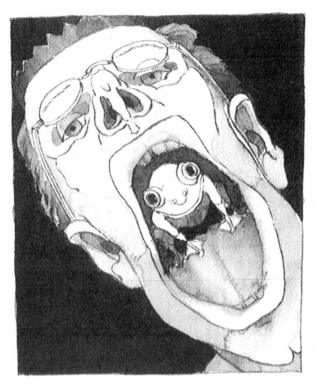

4. He's got a frog in his throat.

Question

State the noncompositional (idiomatic) meaning for expressions 1–4.

1.

2.

3.

4.

5.2 Ambiguous Words

Questions

A. The following words are ambiguous. Some have two meanings; others have more. For each word, define or give a synonym for two meanings. Use your intuitions (not the dictionary).

1. charge

    a.

    b.

2. claim

    a.

    b.

3. park

    a.

    b.

4. soil

    a.

    b.

5. heat

    a.

    b.

B. Provide five examples of words that are ambiguous. Give two different meanings for each one.

1. _____

   a.

   b.

2. _____

   a.

   b.

3. _____

   a.

   b.

4. _____

   a.

   b.

5. _____

   a.

   b.

5.3 Ambiguous Sentences

Question

The following sentences are ambiguous. Provide a paraphrase for each reading or interpretation.

1. The new computer and printer were left at the door.

    a.

    b.

2. The chicken is ready to eat.

    a.

    b.

3. Ringing bells did not annoy him.

    a.

    b.

4. He likes galloping horses.

    a.

    b.

5.4 Homophony and Polysemy

Homophonous words have identical pronunciations but different, not obviously related meanings: *bank* "side of a river" versus *bank* "financial institution." In contrast, a *polysemous word* is a single word that has several closely related meanings: *heart* "(1) organ that supplies blood to the circulatory system; (2) innermost area."

Question

Indicate whether each word below is an instance of homophony or polysemy. Defend your answer in each case by discussing the meanings of the word(s). If the relation is one of polysemy, discuss in what ways the various meanings can be related.

1. accommodation (lodging; anything that meets a need)

2. nail (fingernail or toenail; carpenter's nail)

3. admission (confession; entrance fee)

4. plane (aircraft; flat or level surface)

5. fire (*as in* forest fire; cause someone to become unemployed)

5.5 Evaluative and Emotive Meaning

A word may be associated with more than its literal meaning; it may have emotional connotations as well. Bertrand Russell once offered the following paradigm to illustrate this distinction:

I am firm.
You are obstinate.
He is a pig-headed fool.

The same person might be correctly described by all three terms, but their emotional effects are quite different.

Questions

A. The following triples are further examples of "emotive conjugations." In each case, first state the literal meaning shared by the words and then discuss how they differ in terms of expressed evaluation and emotional impact. Choose three of the following examples to discuss.

    1. tavern, bar, dive

    2. fairer sex, female, broad

3. resign, quit, throw in the towel

4. release, discharge, fire (from a job)

5. meticulous, fussy, nit-picking

6. car, jalopy, heap

7. between jobs, out of work, on the dole

8. separate from, walk out on, desert

9. discriminating, exclusive, snobbish

10. nonsense, baloney, a crock

11. father, dad, old man

12. dead body, corpse, stiff

B. Provide three more sets of examples of "emotive conjugations."

1.

2.

3.

Name _____

Section _____

5.6 Special Topic: Grammaticalization of Semantic Properties

Semantic features or categories that are overtly expressed in the grammar of a language are said to be *grammaticalized*. One example involves plurality. The semantic feature of plurality is grammaticalized in European languages: it appears as a morphological affix on the noun (e.g., the English plural {s, z, ɨz}). In contrast, Asian languages (e.g., Japanese and Chinese) do not have a morphological means to mark plurality. Another example involves the semantic feature of gender. English has lost most of its gender marking, but overt expression of this feature is still part of German, Swedish, French, and Spanish.

The semantic feature of physical shape is grammaticalized in a few Navajo verb roots. A speaker who wants to talk about "giving" or "holding" something in Navajo must choose a verb that indicates the physical properties of the given or held object. A few of the three dozen or so roots for Navajo handling verbs are given below.

	Navajo form	English gloss
1.	yish'aah	"I'm handling one round or bulky object"
2.	yishyį'	"I'm handling one bulky object"
3.	yishjaa'	"I'm handling granular plural objects"
4.	yishjool	"I'm handling noncompact matter (wool, hair, etc.)"
5.	yishką́	"I'm handling something in a vessel"
6.	yishlá	"I'm handling a slender, flexible object"
7.	yishtįįh	"I'm handling a slender, stiff object"
8.	yishtsóós	"I'm handling a flexible, flat object"

In its system of classifiers, Chinese also grammaticalizes physical properties of objects. Some examples of the dozens of these classifiers that appear before nouns are given below. (The diacritics on the morphemes are tone markers.)

	Chinese form	English gloss
1.	yī běn N	"one (classifier) N" (used with books, notebooks)
2.	yī zhāng N	"one (classifier) N" (used with flat, sheetlike objects)
3.	yī gen N	"one (classifier) N" (used with long, slender objects)
4.	yī kè N	"one (classifier) N" (used with plants)
5.	yī kuài N	"one (classifier) N" (used with pieces or lumps of an object)
6.	yī tóu N	"one (classifier) N" (used with things with heads, such as cattle)

Questions

A. There is overlap between the semantic properties that Navajo and Chinese grammaticalize. But now consider how English speakers would refer to certain objects in noun phrase constructions. Fill in an appropriate noun in the following English noun phrases:

1. five _____ of chewing gum (note awkwardness of *five chewing gums*)

2. five _____ of dynamite (note awkwardness of *five dynamites*)

3. five _____ of coal (note awkwardness of *five coals*)

4. five _____ of paper (note awkwardness of *five papers*)

5. five _____ of cattle (note awkwardness of *five cattles*)

6. five _____ of wood (note awkwardness of *five woods*)

B. Supply two more examples of the type of English noun phrase given in question A.

1. _____

2. _____

C. What Navajo root would you use when you handle

1. one piece of uncooked spaghetti   _____

2. one piece of cooked spaghetti   _____

3. a pot of cooked spaghetti   _____

4. a handful of cooked spaghetti   _____

D. Compare and contrast Chinese, Navajo, and English with respect to the importance that the physical shape of objects plays in constructing expressions in each language.

6 Language Variation

6.1 Pronouns: English

Questions

Answer the questions associated with each of the sentences below.

A. 1. Circle the pronoun you would prefer to use in each of the following sentences:

   a. Each senior believes that *they themselves/he himself/she herself* will graduate.
   b. One of the students will surely be on time, won't *they/she/he*?
   c. Each professor prepares *their own/his own/her own* syllabus.

   2. Consider sentences a–c again. Can you imagine situations where using the other pronoun(s) would be more appropriate? Describe them.

B. 1. Complete the sentences below by providing an appropriate tag.

   a. Everyone likes me, _____?

   b. Either John or Jane will go, _____?

   c. A pair of shoes is sitting there, _____?

   d. Everyone likes herself, _____?

2. Were any of your choices problematic? If so, which one(s) and why?

6.2 British English

The following passage contains many words and phrases characteristic of the British English spoken in London. As you read it, try to identify these words and phrases and their meaning in American English; then turn to the question that follows.

Nigel, wearing a smart lounge suit and carrying the inevitable waterproof, descended from the lift of his London flat and posted a letter in the pillarbox. Feeling hungry, Nigel turned into his favourite pub for a pint and some lunch. Bubble and squeak and bangers and mash did not appeal to him today. Instead, he chose plaice with potato. When he ordered, he learned that he had three choices of potato: chips, crisps, and jacket potato. He ordered the jacket potato with a side of courgettes and a slice of wholemeal bread.

After finishing lunch, Nigel walked onto the pavement and stopped to tighten his shoelaces. As he was passing a draper's shop, he suddenly remembered he needed something from a chemist. After having his order filled, he entered a call box, with the intention of calling his friend Llewellyn, since he had forgotten to call before he left his flat. He soon learned that the line was engaged, so he decided that if he was ever to catch Llewellyn up, he should have to take the Tube to Llewellyn's flat. Matters were not so simple since the IRA had phoned in bomb threats so the Tube was running late. The crowds around the buskers in the Tube did not help either.

On top of the Tube problem, it was a bank holiday. The shop assistants were walking with their boyfriends, and many of them were on their way to the cinemas. Matters were rather chaotic on the streets. Animal rights protesters were marching, and one had inadvertently stepped in front of a coach. He was taken to hospital in a critical condition.

Finally Nigel arrived at the flat of his friend Llewellyn. Because the day was bright, they decided to take a trip by train to Brighton and so booked a return. Since the trip was short, they only took monkeynuts and drinks. They read on the way, and a *Times* headline read, "England have won the soccer tournament." Also in the *Times* there was a report on Estuary English, a dialect which was having a major impact on London English. The two friends enjoyed the day and were glad to be out of the bustling city. (Revised from Blancké/Abraham 1935/1953, 49–50)

Translate as much of the passage as you can into American English. Try to guess the meaning of each word that you do not know.

7 Language Change

7.1 Indo-European to English 1

Question

The reconstructed Indo-European (IE) words given in 1–8 are the ancestors of words in Modern English. Both the pronunciation and the meaning have changed. Your task is to determine what the descendant English word is and to describe how the meaning has changed. (Note: Each IE word 1–8 is preceded by *. In the context of historical linguistics, * denotes a reconstructed form, not an ungrammatical form.)

The first step in each case is to apply Grimm's Law, where possible. (For a discussion of Grimm's Law, see *Linguistics*, pp. 324–327.)

Grimm's Law

a. b → p
   d → t
   g → k
b. p → f
   t → θ
   k → x (→ h)
c. bh → b (v)
   dh → d
   gh → g

For example, applied to IE *sab*, meaning "juice," Grimm's Law will yield *sap*, which you can identify as an English word whose meaning has narrowed to mean "juice of a tree."

The consonant changes will apply consistently in words 1–8 (although Modern English will often have *v* in place of *bh*). The vowels, however, undergo much more complicated changes. To determine the descendant English word in each case, replace the IE vowel with different vowels (e.g., *a, e, i, o, u*) until you find an English word that has a meaning related to the meaning of the IE word. For example, the IE word *ghrem* meant "angry." Applying Grimm's Law yields *gr-vowel-m*. Substituting different vowels yields *gram, grem, grim, grom, grum*. The English word *grim* is a likely descendant because it still carries the negative emotional sense found in the IE word.

You need to be mentally flexible for this exercise: experiment and make your best guess about what could be a plausible descendant word. With respect to meaning changes, you will see that the words sometimes narrow in meaning, sometimes broaden, and sometimes drift, both in reference and metaphorically. Note also that some IE verbs end up as English nouns, and some IE nouns end up as English verbs.

1. IE word: *smer*

   Meaning: "grease, fat"

   English word:

   Meaning change:

2. IE word: *gleubh*

   Meaning: "to cut, split off"

   English word:

   Meaning change:

3. IE word: *del(l)*

   Meaning: "to split, carve, cut"

   English word:

   Meaning change:

4. IE word: *gembh*

   Meaning: "tooth"

   English word:

   Meaning change:

5. IE word: *bhrew*

   Meaning: "to boil, ferment"

   English word:

   Meaning change:

6. IE word: *plew*

   Meaning: "to rain"

   English word:

   Meaning change:

7. IE word: *agr(o)* (Note: There is no trace of the *(o)* in Modern English.)

   Meaning: "field"

   English word:

   Meaning change:

8. IE word: *webh

Meaning: "to weave"

English word:

Meaning change:

7.2 Indo-European to English 2

Question

The reconstructed Indo-European (IE) words given in 1–8 are the ancestors of words in Modern English. Both the pronunciation and the meaning have changed. Your task is to determine what the descendant English word is and to describe how the meaning has changed. (Note: Each IE word 1–8 is preceded by *. In the context of historical linguistics, * denotes a reconstructed form, not an ungrammatical form.)

The first step in each case is to apply Grimm's Law, where possible. (For a discussion of Grimm's Law, see *Linguistics*, pp. 324–327.)

Grimm's Law

a. b → p
   d → t
   g → k
b. p → f
   t → θ
   k → x (→ h)
c. bh → b (v)
   dh → d
   gh → g

For example, applied to IE *sab*, meaning "juice," Grimm's Law will yield *sap*, which you can identify as an English word whose meaning has narrowed to mean "juice of a tree."

The consonant changes will apply consistently in words 1–8 (although Modern English will often have *v* in place of *bh*). The vowels, however, undergo much more complicated changes. To determine the descendant English word in each case, replace the IE vowel with different vowels (e.g., *a, e, i, o, u*) until you find an English word that has a meaning related to the meaning of the IE word. For example, the IE word *ghrem* meant "angry." Applying Grimm's Law yields *gr-vowel-m*. Substituting different vowels yields *gram, grem, grim, grom, grum*. The English word *grim* is a likely descendant because it still carries the negative emotional sense found in the IE word.

You need to be mentally flexible for this exercise: experiment and make your best guess about what could be a plausible descendant word. With respect to meaning changes, you will see that the words sometimes narrow in meaning, sometimes broaden, and sometimes drift, both in reference and metaphorically. Note also that some IE verbs end up as English nouns, and some IE nouns end up as English verbs.

1. IE word: *ghrebh

   Meaning: "to dig, bury"

   English word:

   Meaning change:

2. IE word: *bherg

   Meaning: "to buzz, growl"

   English word:

   Meaning change:

3. IE word: *werg

   Meaning: "to do"

   English word:

   Meaning change:

4. IE word: *lendh*

   Meaning: "prairie, heath"

   English word:

   Meaning change:

5. IE word: *kait(o)* (Note: There is no trace of the *(o)* in Modern English.)

   Meaning: "forest, uncultivated land"

   English word:

   Meaning change:

6. IE word: *widh(u)* (Note: There is no trace of the *(u)* in Modern English.)

   Meaning: "tree"

   English word:

   Meaning change:

7. IE word: *bherdh*

   Meaning: "to cut (e.g., to cut wood)"

   English word:

   Meaning change:

8. IE word: *dhelbh

   Meaning: "to dig"

   English word:

   Meaning change:

8 Pragmatics

8.1 Identifying the Message

Look through cartoons A–J and answer the questions that follow.

A.

B.

C.

D.

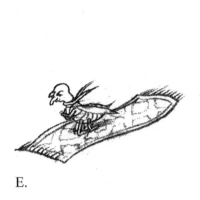

E.

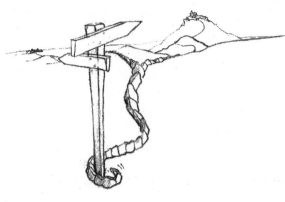

F.

G.

H.

I.

J.

Questions

A. Match each caption with the most appropriate picture. In some cases the caption needs to be modified somewhat to make it appropriate (often this will involve recognizing ambiguities and/or homophony).

Captions   Cartoon

1. pitcher of beer   _____

2. butterballs   _____

3. royal pain   _____

4. hopscotch   _____

5. bird dog   _____

6. catfish   _____

7. fly-by-night   _____

8. a tale of two cities   _____

9. rugby   _____

10. Popeye   _____

B. Discuss possible problems each expression in question A poses for the Message Model of linguistic communication. (See appendix 6 and chapter 9 of *Linguistics* for discussion of the Message Model.)

1.

2.

3.

4.

5.

6.

7.

8.

9.

10.

8.2 Communication Breakdown

Study the cartoon and answer questions A–C.

Questions

A. In *Linguistics*, pp. 372–377, the strategies for literal and direct communication are outlined. At what stage has communication broken down?

B. Given the context of utterance, is it likely that communication would indeed break down? Why or why not?

C. If you argued in question B that it is unlikely that communication would have broken down, then discuss the following question: Does the Message Model have any way of capturing the unlikelihood of communication breaking down in this kind of case? Why or why not? (Review *Linguistics*, pp. 363–370.)

8.3 Literal/Nonliteral Use

Question

A speaker could utter each of the following sentences with the intention of communicating either literally or nonliterally. For at least five of them, state at least two meanings (at least one of which should be literal and at least one of which should be nonliteral) that a speaker could have in mind in using the sentence.

For example: *They are on the way out.* (1) *They* refers to some people who are leaving the room. (2) *They* refers to some shoes that were fashionable last fall but are going out of style.

1. He is on the edge.
2. We're in the same boat.
3. I have my hands full.
4. He didn't get to first base.
5. She broke his heart.
6. That will keep them on their toes.
7. She's losing her grip.
8. He flew off the handle.
9. She blew off steam.
10. Barbara got under her skin.
11. Sue is tied up.
12. He refused to lay his cards on the table.
13. She bit Mary's head off.
14. She gives it to him straight.
15. They beat their brains out.
16. That rings a bell.
17. I got the picture.
18. He'll change his tune.
19. That is right up my alley.
20. He is on the ball.
21. She is standing on her own two feet.
22. He always takes it with a grain of salt.
23. My father is a wet blanket.
24. He will sink or swim.
25. You took the words right out of my mouth.
26. That movie was a real turkey!

1. a.

   b.

2. a.

   b.

3. a.

   b.

4. a.

   b.

5. a.

   b.

8.4 Indirectness

Indirectness in communication involves performing one linguistic act by means of performing another linguistic act. For example, one can perform the act of "ordering" by way of "stating." In answering the questions below, you will be exploring this and other indirect linguistic acts. (See *Linguistics*, pp. 381–385.)

Questions

A. Examine sentences 1–5 and discuss in each case how the speaker could be using the sentence indirectly.

For example: *The bill comes to $10.29.* This sentence is in the declarative mood. (Concerning moods, see appendix 7.) Either it is true that the bill comes to $10.29, or it is false. But one can imagine a situation where someone uttering this sentence (a waiter) could be taken as *requesting* someone else (a customer) to pay the sum of $10.29. That is, it is appropriate on hearing this sentence for the hearer not just to take note of the amount of the bill, but to do something (pay the bill). This is therefore an instance of indirection: performing one act (requesting) by way of another act (stating).

1. I'm hungry.

2. The children are asleep.

3. Are you done yet?

4. What time is it?

5. Is that the radio again?

B. Indirectness can also involve "questioning" by way of "ordering." That is, the sentence is in the imperative mood, but the speaker is also asking for information and is not merely ordering. List some examples of this kind of indirectness.

C. A third form of indirectness involves "stating" by way of "commanding." That is, the sentence is in the imperative mood, but the speaker is also making a statement. List some examples of this kind of indirectness.

8.5 "Unclear Reference" of Pronouns: English

In this exercise you will be trying to figure out the nature of a particular problem: an example of what has been described in a college handbook on writing as "unclear reference" of a pronoun. The handbook characterizes the problem in grammatical terms (see question A). The data in questions B–D challenge this conclusion.

Questions

A. In *Writing: A College Handbook*, the authors offer examples of what they call "unclear reference." One example is as follows:

1. A recent editorial contained an attack on the medical profession. The writer accused them of charging excessively high fees.

The authors provide the following discussion:

Who is meant by the pronoun *them*? From the phrase *medical profession* you may guess that the writer is referring to doctors. But *profession* cannot be the antecedent of *them*, for *them* is plural and *profession* is singular. (Heffernan and Lincoln 1982, 309)

Now consider examples 2 and 3 and answer questions A-1 through A-5.

2. Yesterday, the President announced the decision to send aid to numerous countries in Central America. He went on to say that it was time to help our neighbors in this hemisphere.
3. Yesterday, the White House announced the decision to lift all sanctions. He went on to say that this gesture would set the tone for further negotiations.

1. Who is *he* in example 2?

2. Assume that the noun phrase "antecedent" for *he* is *the White House* in example 3. Who would you guess *he* is? (You may think of several possibilities.)

3. In order to answer question A-2, what kinds of issues must you consider?

4. Examples 2 and 3 are similar in that in each example both the noun phrase "antecedent" (*the President* and *the White House*, respectively) and the pronoun *he* are singular. How are these examples *dissimilar* with respect to determining the reference of *he*?

5. In example 3 *the White House* and the pronoun *he* are both singular, whereas the college handbook describes the problem of determining the reference of *them* in example 1 as a problem of number incompatibility (*profession* is singular, whereas *them* is plural; therefore, *profession* cannot be the "antecedent" for *them*). Is number compatibility between the noun phrase "antecedent" and the pronoun sufficient for determining the reference of the pronoun? Explain, using examples 1 and 3 to back up your arguments.

B. Now consider example 4 and answer questions B-1 through B-4.

4. The office threw a surprise birthday party for the boss. They even gave her a beautiful gift.

1. Who are *they* and how do you know?

2. Is the noun phrase "antecedent" of *they* singular or plural?

3. How does this bear on your discussion in question A-5?

4. Who is *her* being used to refer to? How do you know?

C. The authors of *Writing* suggest that because the pronoun *they* in example 1 is plural, it cannot have the singular *medical profession* as its antecedent, hence that the referent has essentially not been introduced and is therefore indeterminate. Although the reference of the pronoun in this example may indeed be "vague," we must ask whether this problem is to be properly characterized in grammatical terms. Sentence-*internally* we can see that the grammatical requirement of number "agreement" does play a role. Compare example 1 with examples 5 and 6.

5a. *The doctor pays themselves well.
 b. The doctor pays herself well.

6a. *The medical profession pays themselves well.
 b. The medical profession pays itself well.

1. Both examples 5a and 6a are ungrammatical. Identify the problem, keeping in mind examples 1–3.

2. Describe any differences you notice between examples 5a and 6a.

D. Now consider examples 7–9 and answer the questions that follow.

7. They entered the beauty salon and had their hair done.
8. They're flying south for the winter early this year.
9. They won't graduate in four years if they keep up like that.

1. None of the examples in 7–9 provides a noun phrase "antecedent" for the pronoun *they*. Can you guess what the reference of *they* might be in each case?

2. What kind of information did you rely on to make your guesses in question D-1?

3. Does the kind of information you used in question D-2 play a role in helping to identify the reference of the pronoun *they* in example 1? Discuss.

E. In your opinion, is there a problem with the reference of the pronoun *them* in example 1? If your answer is "yes," then discuss why number incompatibility between the noun phrase "antecedent" and the pronoun cannot be the explanation for the problem. If your answer is "no," then explain why the college handbook discussion is inappropriate for you.

8.6 Performative Verbs versus Perlocutionary Verbs

A *performative utterance* describes the act being performed. For example, in the sentence *I predict that it will rain* the performative verb *predict* names the act of predicting; given the right beliefs and intentions, the speaker could, in uttering this sentence, be making a prediction. A *perlocutionary utterance*, on the other hand, is intended to include an effect on the hearer. For example, in the sentence *She persuaded Mary that the argument was solid*, the perlocutionary verb *persuade* describes an act of causing someone to believe or do something (in this case, the act of causing Mary to believe that the argument was solid). In certain syntactic environments the presence of a perlocutionary verb yields an oddity. For example, it is odd to say *I (hereby) persuade you to leave.*

Examine sentences 1–10, and answer the questions that follow.

1. I (hereby) <u>promise</u> to be there.
2. I (hereby) <u>suggest</u> that you leave.
3. I (hereby) <u>convince</u> you that I am right.
4. I (hereby) <u>warn</u> you not to come any closer.
5. I (hereby) <u>incite</u> you to be angry.
6. I (hereby) <u>forbid</u> you to enter this room.
7. I (hereby) <u>inspire</u> you to write beautiful music.
8. I (hereby) <u>amuse</u> you with this story.
9. I (hereby) <u>order</u> you to be quiet.
10. I (hereby) <u>provoke</u> you to punch me.

Questions

A. Which underlined verbs in 1–10 are performative verbs? Give your reasons.

B. Which underlined verbs in 1–10 are perlocutionary verbs? Give your reasons.

C. *I hereby persuade you to leave* is odd. Why is this so? That is, try to *explain* the nature of the oddity.

8.7 Proverbs

Consider the following proverbs and answer questions A and B.

1. Each bird loves to hear himself sing.
2. Friendship is not to be bought at a fair.
3. Fruit ripens not well in the shade.
4. Full bellies make empty skulls.
5. Forbidden fruit is sweet.
6. Fools live poor to die rich.
7. Every tide hath its ebb.
8. Fame is a magnifying glass.
9. Every bird likes its own nest the best.
10. Every bird must hatch its own eggs.
11. What goes around comes around.
12. Can a mouse fall in love with a cat?

Questions

A. How would you paraphrase the intended message behind five of the above proverbs?

   1.

   2.

   3.

4.

5.

B. What kinds of communicative uses of language do proverbs exemplify? In what sense, if any, are proverbs nonliteral? Defend your answer. Discuss at least five of the proverbs.

8.8 Pronoun/Antecedent Agreement: English

The following "agreement principle" can be found in *College Entrance Reviews in English Composition* (revised 1971). Study "Principle 9" and answer the questions that follow.

Principle 9. The number of a pronoun is determined by its antecedent. *Every, each, everyone, anybody, no one*, etc., are singular antecedents. In most instances, in order to avoid awkwardness, *he* or *his* is used to denote both masculine and feminine genders.

1. If *anybody* is looking for an exciting plot, let *him* (not *them*) read this book.
2. *Every one of them* spoke up for *his* own point of view.
3. *Every girl and every boy* in the class is making *his* oral report on the supplementary book today.

Questions

A. Under the view expressed in Principle 9 it is "incorrect" to write a sentence like example 4.

4. Every one of them spoke up for their own point of view.

Nonetheless, examples such as 4 are certainly common these days. Ask your peers whether examples 5 and 6 sound "okay" or not and record your results.

5. Anyone who thinks they can graduate in two years without working is either a genius or out of touch.
6. Somebody in the house left the lights on, didn't they?

B. If consultants say that examples 5 and 6 sound "okay," ask them whether they find any difference between examples 5–6 and examples 7–8 (e.g., differences in use, differences in what the speaker may have in mind, contextual appropriateness). Record your results.

7. Anyone who thinks he can graduate in two years without working is either a genius or out of touch.
8. Somebody in the house left the lights on, didn't he?

C. How does the following quotation from *The First Twelve Months of Life* (1985) bear on the use of *they/them* versus *he/him*? Why would the author include such a comment in the introduction of his book?

A word about gender. Writers on child care may some day succeed in introducing into the language a word that means both "he" and "she." Meantime we will use the convention of the masculine pronoun, but we assure you that unless we are talking about something where sex makes a difference, everything we say about "him" refers to your new daughter as well.

8.9 Major Moods 1: Finnish

The following declarative, interrogative, and imperative sentences are from Finnish, a European language that is not a member of the Indo-European language family. Consider the Finnish sentences and their English translations, and answer questions A–D.

Finnish words exhibit vowel harmony. Thus, the vowels in suffixes vary, depending on the quality of the vowels of the words to which they are attached. In this exercise certain suffixes will therefore appear in two different forms, but they are to be considered as two different versions of the same morpheme. The vowel *ä* is a low front unrounded vowel; the vowel *ö* is a mid front rounded vowel; and the vowel *y* is a high front rounded vowel. A sequence of two identical vowels represents a long vowel of the same quality. (Hint: One way of marking the third person singular subject in Finnish is by lengthening the final vowel of the verb.)

The words in parentheses are optional.

Finnish sentence	English gloss
1. He juovat maitoa hitaasti.	"They are drinking milk slowly."
2. Haluanko (minä) teetä?	"Do I want tea?"
3. Rouva Joki pitää kahvista.	"Mrs. Joki likes coffee."
4. Syö kalaa!	"Eat fish!" (familiar sg.)
5. Juovatko he olutta?	"Are they drinking beer?"
6. (Minä) tarvitsen kupit tänä iltana.	"I need the cups tonight."
7. Juovatko he maitoa hitaasti?	"Are they drinking milk slowly?"
8. Hän haluaa kahvia.	"He/She wants coffee."
9. (Minä) haluan mehua.	"I want (some) juice."
10. (Sinä) juot maitoa tänä iltana.	"You are drinking milk this evening."
11. Pitääkö Rouva Joki kahvista?	"Does Mrs. Joki like coffee?"
12. Haluaako hän kahvia?	"Does he/she want coffee?"
13. Juokaa teetä!	"Drink tea!" (formal sg. or familiar pl.)
14. Tarvitsenko (minä) kupit tänä iltana?	"Do I need cups tonight?"
15. Syökää kalaa!	"Eat fish!" (formal sg. or familiar pl.)
16. Juoko hän nyt olutta?	"Is he/she drinking beer now?"
17. Juo olutta!	"Drink (some) beer!" (familiar sg.)
18. (Minä) haluan teetä.	"I want (some) tea."
19. Hän juo nyt olutta.	"He/She is drinking beer now."
20. Juotko (sinä) maitoa tänä iltana?	"Are you drinking milk tonight?"

21. Haluanko (minä) mehua?	"Do I want (some) juice?"
22. Juo teetä!	"Drink tea!" (familiar sg.)
23. Mikä tämä on?	"What is this?"
24. Tämä on kirja.	"This is a book."
25. Missä kirja on?	"Where is the book?"
26. Missä kahvi on?	"Where is the coffee?"
27. Kuka Tuomari Brown on?	"Who is Judge Brown?"
28. Hän on amerikkalainen diplomaattii.	"He is an American diplomat."
29. Kuka tarvitsee kupit tänä iltana?	"Who needs the cups this evening?"
30. Mitä (partitive case) Tuomari Brown syöö?	"What does Judge Brown eat?"
31. Kenet (objective case) (sinä) tarvitset tänä iltana?	"Who(m) do you need tonight?"

Questions

A. How is person marked in Finnish? That is, by what means are first person (*I*), second person (*you*), and so forth, marked?

B. Compare and contrast the formation of Finnish yes/no questions with the formation of English yes/no questions. Finnish yes/no questions have the same intonation patterns as Finnish declarative sentences. Both have a slight fall in intonation at the end of the sentence.

C. Compare and contrast the formation of Finnish questions that use interrogative pronouns (i.e., pronouns such as *who(m)* and *what*) with the formation of corresponding English questions. Finnish questions with interrogative pronouns have the same intonation patterns as declarative sentences.

D. Compare and contrast the formation of Finnish imperative sentences with that of English imperative sentences.

8.10 Major Moods 2: Copala Trique

Below are sentences illustrating the declarative, interrogative, and imperative moods in Copala Trique, an Otomanguean language spoken in Mexico. Analyze the sentences, and answer questions A–D.

Copala Trique has five phonemic tones, indicated by the numerals 1–5. Vowels marked with 1 (e.g., a^1) are uttered with lowest pitch; those marked with 5 are uttered with highest pitch. Sequences of numbers represent tone contours on individual vowels. For example, a 13 sequence is a tone contour that rises in pitch.

The phonetic symbols used in this exercise are given in the chart in appendix 3. The only symbol that does not appear in the chart is *!*. This symbol represents a feature of articulation, the details of which are too complicated to discuss here (but see Rensch 1978). Familiarity with the phonetic properties of these symbols is not necessary for analyzing the sentences and answering the questions.

Copala Trique sentence	English gloss
1. Kiʔya^{13}h či^3 we^{3}ʔ a^{32}.	"The man will build a house."
2. Turu^{2}no^4! či^3 we^{3}ʔ a^{32}.	"The man will paint a house."
3. Turu^{2}no^4! ša^{3}na^1! we^{3}ʔ a^{32}.	"The woman will paint a house."
4. Turu^{2}no^4! ša^{3}na^1! me^{3}sa^4! a^{32}.	"The woman will paint a table."
5. Kiʔya^{13}h ša^{3}na^1! me^{3}sa^4! a^{32}.	"The woman will make a table."
6. Kiʔya^{13}h či^3 we^{3}ʔ adõh^2.	"The man will surely build a house."
7. Kiʔya^{13}h ša^{3}na^1! me^{3}sa^4! na^{4}ʔ.	"Will the woman make a table?"
8. Turu^{2}no^4! či^3 me^{3}sa^4! na^{4}ʔ.	"Will the man paint a table?"
9. Kiʔya^{13}h ša^{3}na^1! we^{3}ʔ ža^{2}ʔ.	"The woman will build a house, won't she?"
10. Kiʔya^{13}h zo^{3}h we^{3}ʔ a^{32}.	"You all will build a house."
11. Kiʔya^{13}h zo^{3}h we^{3}ʔ a^4.	"Build a house (you all)!"
12. Turu^{2}no^4! zo^{3}h me^{3}sa^4! a^4.	"Paint a table (you all)!"
13. Me^3! zi^5 turn^{2}no^4! we^{3}ʔ ga^2.	"Who will paint a house?"
14. Me^3! zi^5 kiʔya^{13}h me^{3}sa^4! ga^2.	"Who will make a table?"
15. Me^3! ze^{32}! kiʔya^{13}h či^3 ga^2.	"What will the man make?"
16. Me^3! ze^{32}! turu^{2}no^4! ša^{3}na^1! ga^2.	"What will the woman paint?"
17. Kaʔã^{32}h šni^3 šumã^{3}ʔ a^{32}.	"The boy went to town."
18. Kaʔã^{32}h šni^3 šumã^{3}ʔ na^{4}ʔ.	"Did the boy go to town?"
19. Kaʔã^{32}h či^3 šumã^{3}ʔ a^{32}.	"The man went to town."
20. Kaʔã^{32}h či^3 šumã^{3}ʔ na^{4}ʔ.	"Did the man go to town?"
21. Kaʔã^{32}h zo^{1}ʔ šumã^{3}ʔ a^4.	"Go to town!" (sg.)
22. Kanã^{2}h zo^{1}ʔ a^4.	"Weave!" (sg.)

241

23. Kunã²h zo¹ʔ a⁴.   "Run away!" (sg.)
24. Keneʔe³! ša³na¹! (mã³!) šni³ a³².   "The woman saw the boy."
25. Keneʔe³! šni³ (mã³!) ša³na¹! a³².   "The boy saw the woman."
26. Me³! zi⁵ keneʔe³! šni³ ga².   "Who(m) did the boy see?"
27. Me³! zi⁵ keneʔe³! mã³! šni³ ga².   "Who saw the boy?"
28. Me³! zi⁵ kaʔã³²h šumã³ʔ ga².   "Who went to town?"
29. Me³! zi⁵ ča⁴! ru³ci¹ʔ ga².   "Who ate the guava?"
30. Me³! ze³²! keneʔe³! či³ ga².   "What did the man see?"
31. Me³! ze³²! ča⁴! ša³na¹! ga².   "What did the woman eat?"

Questions

A. How are Copala Trique yes/no questions formed?

B. How are Copala Trique questions with interrogative words (in English *who*, *what*, etc., which are called *wh-words*) formed? Compare and contrast the formation of Copala Trique interrogative word questions with the formation of English interrogative word questions.

242

C. How are Copala Trique imperative sentences formed?

D. Discuss the role of word order in Copala Trique. In particular, discuss the absence versus presence of the word $m\tilde{a}^3!$ in sentences 26 and 27, respectively.

8.11 Major Moods 3: Mandarin Chinese

The following sentences illustrate the form that the major moods take in Mandarin Chinese. Analyze the sentences, and answer questions A–D.

Chinese is a tone language; that is, each word is uttered at a characteristic pitch level or with a characteristic pitch change. The tones are indicated with diacritic marks over the vowels. The diacritic ˉ over a vowel indicates a high tone; the diacritic ´ indicates a rising tone; the diacritic ˇ indicates a falling-rising tone; the diacritic ` indicates a falling tone.

	Mandarin Chinese sentence	English gloss
1.	他是教员。 Tā shì jiàoyuán.	"He is a teacher."
2.	(你) 买书! (Nǐ) mǎi shū!	"Buy the books!"
3.	你要什么? Nǐ yào shén-mo?	"What do you want?"
4.	他不到美国来。 Tā bù dào Měi-guo lái.	"He is not coming to America."
5.	王先生来吗? Wáng-Xiānsheng lái ma?	"Is Mr. Wang coming?"
6.	王先生来。 Wáng-Xiānsheng lái.	"Mr. Wang is coming."
7.	你有书吗? Nǐ yǒu shū ma?	"Do you have any books?"
8.	谁卖笔? Sheí mài bǐ?	"Who sells pens?"
9.	我有书。 Wǒ yǒu shū.	"I have books."
10.	(你) 看他们! (Nǐ) kàn tā-men!	"Look at them!"
11.	这是什么? Zhè shì shén-mo?	"What is this?"

12. 我们说中国话。
    Wǒ-men shuō Zhōng-guo-
    huà.   "We speak Chinese."

13. 他们说不说中国话?
    Tā-men shuō bù shuō   "Do they speak Chinese?"
    Zhōng-guo-huà?

14. (你) 说中国话!
    (Nǐ) shuō Zhōng-guo-huà!   "Speak Chinese!"

15. 你们卖不卖笔?
    Nǐ-men mài bù mài bǐ?   "Do you (pl.) sell pens?"

16. 他们卖笔吗?
    Tā-men mài bǐ ma?   "Do they sell pens?"

17. 这是书。
    Zhè shì shū.   "This is a book."

18. (你) 来!
    (Nǐ) lái!   "Come!"

19. 我要买书。
    Wǒ yào mǎi shū.   "I want to buy books."

20. 你看我吗?
    Nǐ kàn wǒ ma?   "Are you looking at me?"

21. 他们不问我们。
    Tā-men bù wèn wǒ-men.   "They didn't ask us."

22. 你们看谁?
    Nǐ-men kàn sheí?   "Who(m) did you (pl.) look at?"

23. 你是不是教员?
    Nǐ shì bù shì jiàoyuán?   "Are you a teacher?"

24. 他们不看我们。
    Tā-men bù kàn wǒ-men.   "They are not looking at us."

25. 我不看你们。
    Wǒ bù kàn nǐ-men.   "I am not looking at you."

Questions

A. 1. Which sentences are in the interrogative mood? That is, which ones are associated with the answerhood condition? List them by number.

2. Describe two ways in which yes/no questions can be formed in Chinese.

3. How are *wh*-questions formed in Chinese? (In English, *wh*-questions are those formed with interrogative pronouns such as *who(m)*, *what*, and so forth.)

B. 1. Which sentences are in the imperative mood? That is, which ones are associated with the compliance condition? List them by number.

2. What is the nature of the grammatical form that signals the imperative mood in Chinese?

C. Which sentences are in the declarative mood? That is, which ones are associated with a truth condition? List them by number.

D. Does word order appear to be important in Chinese? Be specific.

8.12 Pragmatics: Navajo

Some of the following Navajo sentences are acceptable; others (marked with #) are judged by native speakers to be pragmatically unacceptable. In list I both sentences in each pair are acceptable; in lists II and III one sentence in each pair is acceptable and the other is pragmatically odd. Study the sentence pairs in the three lists, and answer the question at the end of the exercise.

There are two differences between the sentences in each pair: a word order change between the first two words (nouns) and a morphological change in the last word (the verb). When the verb begins with *y-* (more precisely, *yi-*), the first noun is the subject. When the verb begins with *bi-*, the second noun is the subject. The pairs of Navajo sentences have been translated into active and passive forms in English, although the sentences translated as English passives are not really passive sentences in Navajo. However, understanding the exact nature of this structural type in Navajo is not important for completing the exercise.

Not all transitive sentences in Navajo have acceptable pairs with the prefixes *yi-* and *bi-*. In list II the *bi-* form yields a pragmatic oddity; in list III the *yi-* form is pragmatically unacceptable.

We have not provided interlinear glosses in lists II and III, since you will know enough about Navajo syntax from studying list I to figure out the meaning of the Navajo words from the English translations.

List I

	Navajo sentence	English gloss
1a.	Łį́į́' dzaanééz yiztał. horse mule kicked	"The horse kicked the mule."
b.	Dzaanééz łį́į́' biztał.	"The mule was kicked by the horse."
2a.	Tł'ízí dibé yizgoh. goat sheep butted	"The goat butted the sheep."
b.	Dibé tł'ízí bizgoh.	"The sheep was butted by the goat."
3a.	Ashkii at'ééd yizts'ǫs. boy girl kissed	"The boy kissed the girl."
b.	At'ééd ashkii bizts'ǫs.	"The girl was kissed by the boy."
4a.	Łééchąą'í mósí yishxash. dog cat bit	"The dog bit the cat."
b.	Mósí łééchąą'í bishxash.	"The cat was bitten by the dog."

5a.	Hastiin asdzání yiyiiłts'ą́.	"The man saw the woman."
	man woman saw	
b.	Asdzání hastiin biiłts'ą́.	"The woman was seen by the man."
6a.	Hastiin ashkii yizloh.	"The man roped the boy."
	man boy roped	
b.	Ashkii hastiin bizloh.	"The boy was roped by the man."
7a.	Ma'ii dibé yiyiisxį́.	"The coyote killed the sheep."
	coyote sheep killed	
b.	Dibé ma'ii biisxį́.	"The sheep was killed by the coyote."
8a.	Másí łééchąą'í yizghas.	"The cat scratched the dog."
	cat dog scratched	
b.	Łééchąą'í másí bizghas.	"The dog was scratched by the cat."

List II

9a.	Łį́į́' tsé yiztał.	"The horse kicked the rock."
b.	#Tsé łį́į́' biztał.	"The rock was kicked by the horse."
10a.	Másí abe' yiłch'al.	"The cat is lapping the milk."
b.	#Abe' másí biłch'al.	"The milk is being lapped by the cat."
11a.	Łééchąą'í łeets'aa' yiłnaad.	"The dog licks the dish."
b.	#Łeets'aa' łééchąą'í biłnaad.	"The dish is licked by the dog."
12a.	Másí naaltsoos yizghas.	"The cat scratches the paper."
b.	#Naaltsoos másí bizghas.	"The paper is scratched by the cat."
13a.	Dibé tł'oh yiłchozh.	"The sheep eats the grass."
b.	#Tł'oh dibé biłchozh.	"The grass is eaten by the sheep."
14a.	Ashkii naaltsoos yizhjih.	"The boy grabbed the book."
b.	#Naaltsoos ashkii bizhjih.	"The book was grabbed by the boy."
15a.	Ashkii tsé'édó'ii yik'idiiltáál.	"The boy stepped on the fly."
b.	#Tsé'édó'ii ashkii bik'idiiltáál.	"The fly was stepped on by the boy."
16a.	Ashkii bįįh yiskah.	"The boy shot the deer."
b.	#Bįįh ashkii biskah.	"The deer was shot by the boy."
17a.	At'ééd dibé yizloh.	"The girl roped the sheep."
b.	#Dibé at'ééd bizloh.	"The sheep was roped by the girl."
18a.	Ashkii gah yisił.	"The boy caught the rabbit."
b.	#Gah ashkii bisił.	"The rabbit was caught by the boy."

List III

19a.	#Tsah asdzání yaa'ííjil.	"The needle stuck the woman."
b.	Asdzání tsah baa'ííjil.	"The woman was stuck by the needle."
20a.	#Béésh ashkii yizhgish.	"The knife cut the boy."
b.	Ashkii béésh bizhgish.	"The boy was cut by the knife."
21a.	#Wóláchíí' hastiin yishish.	"The red ant stung the man."
b.	Hastiin wóláchíí' bishish.	"The man was stung by the red ant."

22a. #Ts'í'ii łį́į' yiyííts'ǫ́ǫz. "The mosquito sucked on the horse."
  b. Łį́į' ts'í'ii bííts'ǫ́ǫz. "The horse was sucked on by the mosquito."

Question

Using the sentences in lists I, II, and III, determine the principle(s) that explain why some of the sentences are unacceptable to Navajo speakers. Be sure to consider the referents of the NPs with respect to the grammatical relations they hold.

9 *Psychology of Language*

9.1 Speech Errors

The phrases and sentences 1–12 illustrate various types of speech errors. Read them, and answer the question that follows. (Some of the examples are taken from Fromkin 1973, Foss and Hakes 1978, and Garrett 1975.)

1. when the bare gets all ground   (as in autumn)
2. Stocks stay up.   (refers to an article of clothing)
3. Seymour sliced the knife with a salami.
4. The early worm gets the bird.
5. Fire fighters are helping to put out blazers.
6. mushmallows   (hint: a fungus and a confection)
7. taddle tennis
8. budbegs
9. foon speeding
10. Make it so the apple has less trees.
11. bridge of the neck
12. The legislature is in its final week of law-breaking.

Question

Discuss the nature of each speech error. Point out whether the error involves phonology, morphology, syntax, or a combination of any of these. That is, what type of unit is involved? What expression was intended in each case?

1. a. Type of error:

   b. Linguistic unit involved:

   c. Intended expression:

2. a.

   b.

   c.

3. a.

   b.

   c.

4. a.

   b.

   c.

5. a.

   b.

   c.

6. a.

   b.

   c.

7. a.

   b.

   c.

8. a.

   b.

   c.

9. a.

   b.

   c.

10. a.

    b.

    c.

11. a.

b.

c.

12. a.

b.

c.

Appendixes

1 How to State Phonological Rules

Several exercises in this workbook require an informal statement of some phonological rule(s). These rules express regularities in the patterning of the sounds in the language in question. In this appendix we will demonstrate how to state such rules, using examples from English.

Consider the following regularity in the pronunciation of vowels in American English: vowels are longer when they appear before voiced consonants than when they appear before voiceless ones. To perceive this difference, utter the words *bit* and *bid* a few times. Notice how much longer the vowel lasts in *bid* than it does in *bit*. The conditioning factor for the lengthening of the vowel in this case is the voiced sound *d* that follows it. A similar length difference appears in the words *tap* and *tab*. Even the already long or tense vowels in pairs such as *beat* and *bead* show a relative length difference.

This lengthening rule of American English vowels is thus a condition on pronunciation that every native speaker has learned. The regularity describing vowel length can be expressed in statement 1.

1. A vowel is lengthened before a voiced consonant.

This statement can also be expressed in the following more concise notation:

2. [vowel] → [lengthened] / _____ [voiced consonants]

And this statement in turn is an instance of a more abstract rule pattern:

3. A → B / C _____ D

Rule pattern 3 can be read as follows: "A is realized as B when it appears in an environment where it is immediately preceded by C (i.e., A is to the right of C) and immediately followed by D (i.e., A is to the left of D)."

In other words:

→   is to be read "is realized as" or "becomes."
/   is to be read "in the environment of."
_____ (called the *focus bar*) specifies the relative position of the segment subject to the rule, in this case A, to the segments conditioning the rule, in this case C and D.

The pattern given in rule schema 3 is characteristic of most of the phonological regularities found in this workbook and is typical of the pattern of phonological rules found in the world's languages.

In the case of the American English vowel-lengthening rule, A is any vowel, B is the specification "lengthening," C is lacking, and D is a voiced consonant. This is the form given as rule statement 2.

An example of a phonological rule in which both C and D must be present is the Flap Rule (see *Linguistics*, pp. 92–93), which specifies that a flap, [ɾ], replaces a [t] when it occurs between vowels and when the first vowel is stressed:

4. [t] → [ɾ] / [V́] _____ [V]

This rule is characteristic of modern American English. It accounts for the pronunciation of *pitted* [pʰírɨd] and *hottest* [hɔ́rəst]. It is, then, an example of rule template 3 in which A is *t*, B is the flapped *ɾ*, C is a stressed vowel, and D is another vowel.

There are also rules in which part C of the conditioning environment is present and part D is absent. An example is the Plural Rule of English (see *Linguistics*, pp. 86–90).

2 The Role of Distinctive Features in Phonological Rules

For the most part, phonological rules can be expressed with a formula of the form
A → B / C ____ D, where the alphabetic symbols represent one or more
phonemes (see appendix 1). However, since the smallest isolatable units of a
language's sound system are not phonemes (or their allophones), but the distinctive
features that compose the phonemes, phonological rules are better stated in terms
of these distinctive features.

To begin to see why this is so, let us return to the Vowel-Lengthening Rule of
English discussed in appendix 1:

1. English Vowel-Lengthening Rule
   [vowel] → [lengthened] / ____ [voiced consonants]

The form of rule 1 already anticipates the point that such rules are best expressed
in terms of the distinctive features that make up the phonemes that participate in
the phonological regularities of a language. Contrast rule 1 with the same rule
expressed in terms of phonemes:

2. $\begin{bmatrix} \text{I} \\ \varepsilon \\ \text{æ} \\ \Lambda \\ \text{ɑ} \\ \text{ɔ} \\ \text{ʊ} \\ \text{i} \\ \text{eɪ} \\ \text{aɪ} \\ \text{u} \\ \text{oʊ} \\ \text{aʊ} \\ \text{ɔɪ} \end{bmatrix} \rightarrow \begin{bmatrix} \text{ɪ:} \\ \varepsilon\text{:} \\ \text{æ:} \\ \Lambda\text{:} \\ \text{ɑ:} \\ \text{ɔ:} \\ \text{ʊ:} \\ \text{i:} \\ \text{e:ɪ} \\ \text{a:ɪ} \\ \text{u:} \\ \text{o:ʊ} \\ \text{a:ʊ} \\ \text{ɔ:ɪ} \end{bmatrix} / ____ \begin{bmatrix} \text{b} \\ \text{d} \\ \text{g} \\ \text{m} \\ \text{n} \\ \text{ŋ} \\ \text{v} \\ \text{ð} \\ \text{z} \\ \text{ʒ} \\ \text{dʒ} \\ \text{ɹ} \\ \text{l} \end{bmatrix}$

Although rules 1 and 2 account for the same data, rule 1 expresses the
generalization that explains *why* the phonemes that are listed in rule 2 pattern
together. For example, as far as the list of phonemes in rule 2 is concerned, we
could replace *z* with *s* on the right (part D of the context), and rule 2 would be
almost the same in form and complexity. Only rule 1 explains why *s* is excluded in
part D of the rule, however: *s* is a voiceless consonant, and all of the other
consonants in the right-hand list in rule 2 are voiced. Rule 1 *rules out* the presence
of *s* in the list of conditioning phonemes—exactly the right result.

In addition, the formulation of rule 1 makes unnecessary the large number of
individual statements that would be required if we were forced (for some reason)
to make all of the allophonic statements for each phoneme individually. Clearly,
we would not want to have a rule stating that the phoneme /ɪ/ has a variant [ɪ:]
before *d*, *n*, *z*, and so forth. It is not the case that each phoneme of a language
must have its own individual sets of rules that determine its allophones; rather,

rules that specify allophonic detail are general and may be applicable to several phonemes.

As it is now stated, rule 1 is not precisely in the form in which phonological rules must be written. Two changes are needed: first, the specifications + (plus) and − (minus) must be added to the features; and second, a more precise and empirically justified set of distinctive features must be employed. For justification of the intrinsic content of a more appropriate set of distinctive features, see *Linguistics*, pp. 110–118.

We have already tacitly assumed that the features that make up phonemes are binary. That is, each one can have two values: + and −. For example, the feature of voicing can appear either as voiced ([+voiced]) or as voiceless ([−voiced]). There are two reasons for claiming that distinctive features are binary. First, people perceive features categorically—as being either present or not present—and not as a continuum. If a voiced sound—for example, *b*—is produced with some degree of nasalization, listeners perceive either *m* or *b*—they do not perceive some intermediate third sound. In experiments with synthetic speech, for example, subjects will hear either *mad* or *bad*, depending on the amount of nasality that was supplied in synthesizing the initial consonant. Second, only the absolute values + and − are needed for the proper statement of phonological rules. For example, one never has to state that a phonological rule is applicable if *m* has 3 degrees of nasality, *n* has 2 degrees of nasality, *ŋ* has 4 degrees of nasality, and so forth. If the class of nasal phonemes participates in a rule, only the feature [+nasal] (or [−nasal]) is needed to specify that class.

One other point needs to be made before we state rule 1 in its final form. The consonants in part D of rule 1 all share the property of being voiced; that is, they all have the feature [+voiced]. These consonants thus constitute a *natural class* of phonemes that can be defined by a small number of distinctive features. (See *Linguistics*, pp. 121–124, for additional discussion and motivation of the notion "natural class.") Several problems in this workbook (exercises 3.3–3.6) require a phonological rule to be stated in terms of the *distinctive features that define a natural class of phonemes*. Your task in these cases is to find a set of features that will include all of the phonemes in the class and exclude all of the other phonemes in the language. A chart listing the distinctive features of all the phonemes needed for the exercises has been included in appendix 4. (For a description of the features themselves, see *Linguistics*, pp. 114–118.)

To return to rule 2: The phonemes that participate in this rule can be found in appendix 4. It is similar, then, to the intermediate stages you will go through in formulating your rules in exercises 3.3–3.6. In rule 2 the feature that uniquely specifies all of the sounds that undergo vowel lengthening is the feature [+syllabic]. The features that uniquely specify the set of phonemes to the right of the focus bar (part D of the rule) are [+consonantal] and [+voiced]. The feature that specifies part B of the rule is [+long]. (Since there is some question concerning how the feature [+long] is to be represented in phonological theory, it has not been listed as a feature in appendix 4.)

The final form of the rule can now be given as follows:

3. English Vowel-Lengthening Rule (final form)

$$[\text{+syllabic}] \rightarrow [\text{+long}] \, / \, \underline{\hspace{1cm}} \begin{bmatrix} \text{+consonantal} \\ \text{+voiced} \end{bmatrix}$$

In other words, phonemes that possess the feature [+syllabic] are assigned the feature [+long] whenever they appear before phonemes having the features [+consonantal] and [+voiced].

The answers to exercises 3.3–3.6 require statements similar to rule 3. When only a single phoneme appears in one part of the rule, however, you are usually not required to give its unique distinctive feature specification, although this would be required in a more technical statement of the rule.

3 Transcription Key

Consonants

		Bilabial	Labio-dental	Inter-dental	Dental, alveolar	Retroflex	Alveo-palatal	Palatal	Velar	Glottal
Stops	voiceless	p			t	ṭ		c	k	ʔ
	voiced	b			d	ḍ		ɟ	g (g)	
Fricatives	voiceless	ɸ	f	θ	s	ṣ	ʃ (š)		x	h
	voiced	β	v	ð	z	ẓ	ʒ (ž)		ɣ	
Affricates	voiceless				tˢ		tʃ (č)			
	voiced				dᶻ		dʒ (ǰ)			
Nasals		m			n	ṇ	ɲ (ñ)		ŋ	
Liquids	lateral				l					
	nonlateral				r	ṛ				
Glides		w(ʍ)			ɹ		j (y)			

Additional symbols

Cʸ = palatalized consonant (for example, tʸ = palatalized t)

C' = glottalized consonant (for example, t' = glottalized (or ejective) t)

' = glottal stop in some transcription systems

Vowels, unrounded

		Front	Central	Back
High	Tense	i		
	Lax	ɪ	ɨ	
Mid	Tense	e (eɪ)		
	Lax	ɛ	ʌ(ə)	
Low		æ		ɑ (aɪ, aʊ)

Vowels, rounded

		Front	Central	Back
High	Tense	y (ü)		u
	Lax			ʊ
Mid	Tense	ø (ö)		o (oʊ, ɔɪ)
	Lax			ɔ

Additional symbols

V: = long vowel

Ṽ = nasalized vowel

r̩ = syllabic r. A tick mark under certain resonants (r, l, m, etc.) indicates that the consonant functions as a vowel-like sound.

There are two ways of transcribing the long vowels of English: i, e, o, u and i, eɪ, oʊ, u. Because diphthongs cannot be represented as a single point on a vowel chart, we represent them in terms of the position of their initial vowel.

4 Chart of Distinctive Features

Sonorant consonants and glides: (−syllabic, +sonorant)

	m	n	ṇ	ɲ (ñ)	ŋ	l	r* (ɹ)	ṛ	j (y)	w	h	ʔ
Consonantal	+	+	+	+	+	+	+/−	+	−	−	−	−
Nasal	+	+	+	+	+	−	−	−	−	−	−	−
Lateral	−	−	−	−	−	+	−	−	−	−	−	−
Continuant	−	−	−	−	−	+	+	+	+	+	+	−
Distributed	−	−	−	+	−	−	−	−	−	−	−	−
Coronal	−	+	+	+	−	+	+	+	+	−	−	−
Retroflex	−	−	+	−	−	−	−	+	−	−	−	−
Labial	+	−	−	−	−	−	−	−	−	+	−	−
Anterior	+	+	−	−	−	+	+	+	−	−	−	−
High	−	−	−	+	+	−	−	−	+	+	−	−
Back	−	−	−	−	+	−	−	−	−	+	−	−
Strident	−	−	−	−	−	−	−	−	−	−	−	−

Obstruents: (−syllabic, +consonantal, −sonorant)

−Voiced:	p	ɸ	f	θ	t	s	t^s	ṭ	ṣ	ʃ (š)	tʃ (č)	c	k	x
+Voiced:	b	β	v	ð	d	z	d^z	ḍ	ẓ	ʒ (ž)	dʒ (ǰ)	ɟ	g (g)	ɣ
Nasal	−	−	−	−	−	−	−	−	−	−	−	−	−	−
Lateral	−	−	−	−	−	−	−	−	−	−	−	−	−	−
Continuant	−	+	+	+	−	+	−	−	+	+	−	−	−	+
Distributed				−	−	−	−	−	−	+	+			
Coronal	−	−	−	+	+	+	+	+	+	+	+	−	−	−
Retroflex	−	−	−	−	−	−	−	+	+	−	−	−	−	−
Labial	+	+	+	−	−	−	−	−	−	−	−	−	−	−
Anterior	+	+	+	+	+	+	+	−	−	−	−	−	−	−
High	−	−	−	−	−	−	−	−	−	+	+	+	+	+
Back	−	−	−	−	−	−	−	−	−	−	−	−	+	+
Strident	−	−	+	−	−	+	+	−	+	+	+	−	−	−
Delayed release (affricate)	−	−	−	−	−	−	+	−	−	−	+	−	−	−

* r is [−consonantal] in English but [+consonantal] in other languages.

Vowels: (+syllabic, −consonantal, +sonorant)

	i	ɪ	ɨ	y (ü)	u	ʊ	e	ɛ	ʌ (ə)	o	ø (ö)	ɔ*	æ	ɑ
High	+	+	+	+	+	+	−	−	−	−	−	−	−	−
Low	−	−	−	−	−	−	−	−	−	−	−	+/−	+	+
Back**	−	−	+	−	+	+	−	−	+	+	−	+	−	+
Round	−	−	−	+	+	+	−	−	−	+	+	+	−	−
Tense	+	−			+	−	+	−		+	+			

* This symbol represents a low back rounded vowel in English. In other languages it represents a mid lax back rounded vowel.

** The central and back vowels given in the transcription key (appendix 3) all have the feature [+back].

5 Some Phrase Structure Rules for English

For discussion of phrase structure rules, see *Linguistics*, chapter 5.

1. S → NP (Aux) VP
2. NP → (Art) N (PP)
3. NP → (Poss) N
4. Poss → NP Poss-Affix
5. NP → NP Conjunction NP
6. NP → (Q) N (Mod)
7. VP → V $\left(\left\{ \begin{array}{c} NP \\ S \end{array} \right\} \right)$
8. VP → V (NP) (PP)
9. V → V Particle
10. PP → P NP

Aux = Auxiliary
Art = Article
Poss = Possessive
Q = Quantifier
Mod = Modifier
P = Preposition

6 The Message Model of Linguistic Communication

The Message Model of linguistic communication may be described as follows:

A speaker has some message in mind that she wants to communicate to a hearer. The speaker then produces some expression from the language that encodes the message as its meaning. Upon hearing the beginning of the expression, the hearer begins identifying the incoming sounds, syntax, and meanings; then, using her knowledge of language, she composes these meanings in the form of a successfully decoded message. (*Linguistics*, p. 364)

According to the Message Model, then, the question "How does successful communication work?" can be answered as follows:

Linguistic communication is successful if the hearer receives the speaker's message. It works because messages have been conventionalized as the meaning of expressions, and by sharing knowledge of the meaning of an expression, the hearer can recognize a speaker's message—the speaker's communicative intention. (*Linguistics*, p. 369)

See pages 366–370 of *Linguistics* for a discussion of problems that arise with the Message Model.

7 Major Moods

Expressions of a language can be used to perform the following *speech acts:*

1. Questioning
2. Stating, promising, threatening, predicting
3. Requesting, commanding, ordering, pleading

Correlated with each type of speech act is a *condition of satisfaction:*

1. Questioning is correlated with an "answerhood condition."
2. Stating is correlated with a "truth condition."
3. Requesting is correlated with a "compliance condition."

Each speech act/satisfaction condition pair is in turn correlated with a *form*. The resulting triple is termed an instance of a particular *mood:*

1. Questioning is associated, directly, with the interrogative mood.
2. Stating is associated with the declarative mood.
3. Requesting is associated with the imperative mood.

The following are examples, in English, of the three major moods.

Interrogative mood

1. Will he leave?

The person who utters sentence 1 is performing a speech act of questioning, which requires the hearer to supply the speaker with the answer. That is, the answerhood condition is operative.

Declarative mood

2. John left the room.

Taken as a statement (i.e., as an instance of the speech act of stating), sentence 2 is either true or false. Truth or falsity is the relevant notion here—the truth condition is operative.

Imperative mood

3. Leave the room!

Taken as an order (i.e., as an instance of the speech act of ordering), sentence 3 involves compliance. The hearer is to do what the sentence describes (in this case, the speaker intends that the hearer leave the room). The compliance condition is operative.

For each language the speech act/satisfaction condition/form pairing is different. That is, different languages choose different syntactic, morphological, and/or phonological (intonation) devices to signal the major moods.

8 Index of Languages

Language	Language family	Principal area where spoken	Exercise
Chinese	Sino-Tibetan	China	5.6, 8.11
Copala Trique	Otomanguean	Mexico	8.10
Dyirbal	Pama-Nyungan	Australia	4.13
Finnish	Finno-Ugric	Finland	8.9
French	Indo-European	Europe	3.9, 3.10
German	Indo-European	Europe	4.9
Irish	Indo-European	Ireland	4.16
Japanese	Japanese	Japan	2.6, 3.5, 3.6, 4.14, 4.15, 4.24, 4.25
Korean	Korean	Korea	3.2
Nahuatl	Uto-Aztecan	Mexico	4.19
Navajo	Athabascan	North America	5.6, 8.12
Russian	Indo-European	Russia	1.8, 4.23
Spanish	Indo-European	Spain, New World	2.3
Swahili	Niger-Congo	Africa	4.18
Tamil	Dravidian	India	4.10
Telugu	Dravidian	India	4.17
Tohono O'odham	Uto-Aztecan	North America	1.6, 1.7, 3.3, 4.11
Turkish	Ural-Altaic	Turkey	1.9
Yaqui	Uto-Aztecan	North America	4.12
Zoque	Mixe-Zoque	Mexico	3.4

Bibliography

Akmajian, A., R. A. Demers, A. K. Farmer, and R. M. Harnish. 2001. *Linguistics: An introduction to language and communication.* 5th ed. Cambridge, Mass.: MIT Press.

Andrews, R. 1975. *Introduction to classical Nahuatl.* Austin: University of Texas Press.

Beythan, H. 1943. *Praktische Grammatik der Tamilsprache.* Leipzig: Otto Harrassowitz.

Blancké, W. W. 1935. *General principles of language and experiences in language.* Boston: D. C. Heath and Co. [Revised edition 1953, ed. R. Abraham.]

Brauner, S., and J. Bantu. 1964. *Lehrbuch des Swahili.* Leipzig: VEB Verlag Enzyklopädie.

Burgess, A. 1962. *A clockwork orange.* New York: Ballantine Books.

Caplan, F. 1985. *The first twelve months of life.* New York: Bantam Books.

Cook, S. J., and R. W. Suter. 1980. *The scope of grammar: A study of modern English.* New York: McGraw-Hill.

Copi, I. M. 1982. *Introduction to logic.* New York: Macmillan.

Escalante, F. 1990. Voice and argument structure in Yaqui. Doctoral dissertation, University of Arizona.

Foss, D., and D. Hakes. 1978. *Psycholinguistics: An introduction to the psychology of language.* Englewood Cliffs, N.J.: Prentice-Hall.

Foster, H. 1982. The problem of pluralism.

Fromkin, V. 1973. Slips of the tongue. *Scientific American* 229.6, 110–116.

Fromkin, V., and R. Rodman. 1988. *An introduction to language.* 4th ed. New York: Holt, Rinehart and Winston.

Fromm, H. 1982. *Finnische Grammatik.* Heidelberg: Carl Winter Universitätsverlag.

Garrett, M. 1975. The analysis of sentence production. In G. H. Bower, ed., *The psychology of learning and motivation*, vol. 9. New York: Academic Press.

Halle, M., and G. N. Clements. 1982. *Problem book in phonology.* Cambridge, Mass.: MIT Press.

Heffernan, J. A., and J. E. Lincoln. 1982. *Writing: A college handbook.* New York: W. W. Norton.

Hurford, J. R., and B. Heasley. 1983. *Semantics: A coursebook.* Cambridge: Cambridge University Press.

Joyce, J. 1946. *Collected poems.* New York: Viking Press.

Lehtinen, M. 1962. *Basic course in Finnish.* Bloomington: Indiana University Press, and The Hague: Mouton.

Myachina, E. N. 1981. *The Swahili language: A descriptive grammar.* London: Routledge and Kegan Paul.

Orgel, J. R. 1971. *College entrance reviews in English composition.* Cambridge, Mass.: Educators Publishing Service.

Phys, E. 1928. *A dictionary of quotations and proverbs.* London: J. M. Dent and Sons, and New York: E. P. Dutton and Co.

Rensch, C. R. 1978. Ballistic and controlled syllables in Otomanguean languages. In A. Bell and J. B. Hooper, eds., *Syllables and segments.* Amsterdam: North-Holland.

Subrahmanyam, P. 1974. *An introduction to modern Telugu.* Annamalainagar, India: Sivakami Printers.

Townsend, C. E. 1975. *Russian word-formation.* Cambridge, Mass.: Slavica Publishers.

Trager, C. L., and H. L. Smith, Jr. 1957. *An outline of English structure*. Studies in Linguistics, Occasional Papers 3. Reprinted. Washington, D.C.: American Council of Learned Societies.

Walker, J. 1936. *The rhyming dictionary of the English language*. New York: E. P. Dutton and Co.

Watkins, C. 1969. Indo-European roots. In W. Morris, ed., *The American Heritage dictionary of the English language*. Boston: American Heritage Publishing Company and Houghton Mifflin Company.

Wonderly, W. 1951. Zoque II: Phonemes and morphemes. *International Journal of American Linguistics (IJAL)* 17, 105–123.

Zepeda, O. 1983. *A Papago grammar*. Tucson: University of Arizona Press.